COOK
SHARE
EAT
VEGAN

COOK
SHARE
EAT
VEGAN

DELICIOUS PLANT-BASED RECIPES FOR EVERYONE

ÁINE CARLIN

MITCHELL BEAZLEY

CONTENTS

MY VEGAN KITCHEN

For as long as I can remember the kitchen has been the social focal point of any place I have ever called home – whether the Irish childhood home that gave me Sunday dinners and creamy rice puddings, the London one I briefly shared with friends in my mid-twenties (with its array of varying tastes and preferences), or the current Penzance place that my husband and I have lovingly cultivated. Each has shown me the power food possesses in bringing us together, no matter what cultural background we may come from, or indeed what dietary requirements we might have. For me, veganism has opened so many doors and has brought me so much joy and inner peace, it makes sense that I want to share it with my friends and family. Nothing brings me more happiness than creating an abundance of wholesome, seasonal food that will perfectly set the stage for any gathering, no matter how fancy or humble.

Of course, I like to treat every meal as an event, which is why the dishes in this book are suitable for a variety of occasions, even if those occasions happen to involve being curled up on the sofa on a gloomy Wednesday with only one person to feed – yourself. You could say my raison d'etre is to ensure food (and the cooking thereof) is both straightforward and delicious in equal measure. I've long since held the belief that food created under any sort of duress (self-inflicted or otherwise) never tastes quite as good as a dish made with ease and love. And while the odd recipe might require a little more effort, you can rest assured that nothing in this book is beyond even the most nervous cook's capabilities.

Keeping things simple means that you'll find similar ingredients, sauces, dressings and food combinations rearing their familiar heads at various points throughout the chapters of this book. There are many practical reasons for having staples at the heart of your repertoire – I find it gives me the ability to improvise freely around what I like to call my 'fundamental foodie structure'. My 'Goes-With-Everything' Tahini Sauce (*see* page 151) is a perfect example: due to its endless versatility, I find myself tweaking it to accompany both sweet and savoury dishes on a regular basis, without it ever feeling predictable or dull. Likewise, you'll notice I have a thing for black beans and avocado (*see* the Chimichangas on page 76 or my crazy good Baked Potato Nachos on page 158 for proof), and try as I might to break this addiction, somehow I still gravitate to this naturally delicious duo and never once regret it.

I like to think that many of my recipes are simply jumping-off points for people who are seeking a little encouragement when it comes to plant-based cooking. My aim is always to sway the focus away from the 'vegan' tagline and instead bring the food itself to the fore. Creating beautiful, colourful, nutritious food that never fails to raise an approving smile is absolutely at the core of my cooking. And yes, it just happens to be vegan too.

THE BASICS

While veganism is making its way to the mainstream that doesn't mean there aren't still a few helpful tips and tricks that can make your life a little easier. So before you get cracking with the recipes, these are the basics that need covering.

HOW AND WHY TO SOAK NUTS

You'll notice that nuts play a vital role in my plant-based lifestyle, and rightly so. Not only are they important for a balanced, nutritious diet, providing us with essential fats and various amounts of protein and calcium, but they also happen to be fabulously versatile. To get the best out of your nuts you'll want to soak them beforehand – simply place your nuts in a bowl and pour over enough filtered water to completely cover them. Don't panic about this, I simply mean water from a filter jug or filter tap, not bottled water, but if you don't have a water filter then regular tap water will do.

I usually soak my nuts overnight but certain types are more susceptible to 'turning' – for example, cashew nuts can become slimy if left to soak for too long, so I try to use those within an 8-hour period or thereabouts. It goes without saying that the harder the nut the longer the soak, so almonds, macadamias and Brazil nuts really do benefit from being left for a few extra hours. Once you've finished soaking, simply drain the nuts and rinse them under cold running water before using them as you like.

> **QUICK SOAK TIP!** At a pinch you can cover your nuts with freshly boiled water and set them aside for 30 minutes. This soak won't be quite as effective but it will still soften the nuts enough to make them easier to blend.

PLANT MILKS

I make a variety of plant milks on a weekly rotation, using the same basic recipe. For milks I've settled on the three-to-one ratio – that means three parts liquid to one part nut. You could make the nuts stretch a little further by opting for a four-to-one ratio (which will still be very creamy and almost akin to the consistency of semi-skimmed milk) but I just adore the rich deliciousness of slightly thicker plant milks. These also tend to work much better in coffee and tea. Speaking of which, you'll soon notice that some plant milks tend to curdle more than others in hot drinks, but I've never had an issue with oat milk, which makes for a particularly wonderful creamer. Temperature usually plays a role in why plant milks curdle so I find it helps to let the coffee or tea cool slightly first, as well as heating the milk a tad before using. These are things you'll soon get the hang of, so even if it fails once you'll eventually find the knack.

Because there's no need to soak oats that usually puts oat milk at the top of the pile for me, but I also adore almond milk, which definitely comes a very close second. Cashew milk is a favourite for many because it doesn't necessarily need straining, although I do so anyway because I like my milks super-smooth. And when it comes to straining, nut milk bags can be obtained easily online and are specifically designed for straining nut milks without the faff of using a muslin cloth (though they do exactly the same job). Plant

milks do sometimes separate in the refrigerator (it's normal, don't panic) so always give them a good shake before using. It's also wise to invest in a couple of glass bottles – I favour the traditional Weck brand but any BPA-free bottle will suffice. Enough babble, on to the milk…

BASIC PLANT MILK RECIPE
MAKES APPROX. 750ML

100g soaked and drained nuts (*see* opposite)
   or un-soaked rolled oats
750ml filtered water
1.   Place the nuts (or oats) and water in a blender and blend for up to 1 minute until smooth. A high-speed blender will produce smoother results, but a regular blender is fine.

2.   Strain through a nut milk bag or some muslin cloth to collect any unwanted pulp.
3.   Transfer to a sterilized glass bottle and refrigerate for up to 4 days.

> FLAVOUR TIP! If you want to flavour your nut milk, the possibilities are endless. From time to time I like adding a pinch of pink Himalayan salt, a little vanilla extract or maple syrup or a touch of ground cinnamon.

DAIRY-FREE CREAMS

Creams are a mainstay in my kitchen, in both savoury and sweet dishes. How creamy you require them to be will be reflected in the amount of liquid added – soured cream will need slightly more water than, say, cream for a cheesecake. Once you've achieved the desired consistency, these creams become a great backdrop for an array of flavours, such as the chipotle soured cream that accompanies my Sweet Potato Hash Browns (*see* page 86). Creamy fillings for dairy-free desserts such as the Matcha & Lime Pie (*see* page 192) can also be easily altered to suit: if you're not so keen on citrus, for example, then add a heaped tablespoon of raw cacao to the mix instead for a wonderfully rich alternative. Here are a few of my essential everyday recipes:

CASHEW SOURED CREAM
MAKES APPROX. 250ML

I typically use this cashew cream recipe as a base, adding various spices and pastes to create an entirely different vibe each time. It is wonderfully versatile and a great one to have up your sleeve. For a sweeter version, omit the cider vinegar.

150g soaked cashew nuts (*see* page 8), drained
125ml filtered water
juice of ½ lemon
1 teaspoon cider vinegar
½ teaspoon sea salt flakes

Place everything in a blender and blend until smooth, scraping down the sides from time to time. With plant creams it is crucial you get them as smooth as possible – they will go through several stages before they get there, so persevere until you reach the desired consistency. Check for seasoning and refrigerate until needed.

ALMOND POURING CREAM
MAKES APPROX. 350ML

100g soaked blanched almonds (*see* page 8), drained
250ml filtered water, plus extra if necessary
3 tablespoons maple syrup
1 teaspoon vanilla extract
pinch of sea salt flakes

Add everything to a blender and blend until you achieved a pouring (single cream) consistency, adding a little more water if necessary.

MACADAMIA CREAM
MAKES APPROX. 200ML

Macadamia cream can be used to great effect in both sweet and savoury dishes. Once blended it becomes light and fluffy and is delicate enough to absorb a variety of flavours. For savoury creams I stick to brighter notes by adding a little lemon or lime juice (cashew cream is much more suited to robust flavours) and I usually avoid adding any sort of vinegar. If I want to sweeten things up I add agave nectar or maple syrup (and a touch of natural extract such as lemon or vanilla) but I try not to overdo it because macadamias have a wonderful natural sweetness that shouldn't be overshadowed. They might be pricey, but for an occasional treat they are worth the investment.

100g macadamias, soaked
75ml filtered water, plus extra if necessary
¼ teaspoon sea salt flakes

Add everything to a blender and blend, scraping down the sides from time to time and adding a splash or two more water if necessary, until light and fluffy.

HOW TO TOAST NUTS & SEEDS

In order to get the best out of nuts, you sometimes have to give them a little encouragement in the oven or on the hob. It's also the easiest way to remove those stubborn skins. Once you remove the nuts from the heat, place them in a clean tea towel and rub vigorously – the skins should come off effortlessly.

For a more even toasting – even for delicate nuts such as flaked almonds or coconut flakes – the oven works best. I arrange the nuts on a baking sheet in an even layer and toast them in an oven preheated to 200°C (180°C fan), Gas Mark 6 for 10–15 minutes, or until golden and crunchy, shaking the sheet occasionally and keeping an eye on them to ensure they don't burn (this can happen very quickly). When toasting nuts on the hob I place them in a dry frying pan set over a medium heat and toast them for up to 5 minutes, tossing them lightly from time to time.

A NOTE ON SUGARS

I don't discriminate when it comes to sugar. While on a daily basis I try to stick to the unrefined variety, I see no harm in using caster, granulated or light brown sugar in baking as and when needed – my Vegan Pavlova (see page 226) simply doesn't work with liquid sweeteners. I also try not to place too much (if any) guilt on such things because, really, life's too short. If it's consumed in moderation then I don't think we should be overly concerned.

A NOTE ON FLOURS

I use a wide variety of flours in my recipes, everything from buckwheat through to spelt, rye, rice and gram (chickpea) – and, yes, even good old regular white flour, which you will see crop up in a number of dishes here and there. If you have a gluten-intolerance issue then substitute it with a suitable alternative (there are a wide variety now on the market) but I'm perfectly happy to use and eat all flours, even those now deemed 'unhealthy' by some. I always endeavour to buy organic and usually make my baked goods in small batches, so I never feel as if I'm overdoing it on the flour front anyway. After all, bread is life – or at least in my world it is.

LET'S TALK ABOUT TOFU

I want to address any queries or reservations you might have about tofu right away – while I understand that you might have put bean curd firmly in the 'bleurgh' category, I'm here to gently right those wrongs and put it back on the menu. Tofu will readily absorb any flavours you throw at it. The longer you marinate it, the more flavourful it will become – just remember to season, season, season! Then it's just a matter of cooking it to your liking and adding it to your favourite dish.

To keep things simple there are, generally speaking, two main varieties of tofu on the market – firm and silken. Firm tofu is typically reserved for savoury dishes and really benefits from being 'pressed'. Simply drain the tofu block and pat it dry before placing it in a shallow bowl. Put a plate on top and weigh it down with several cans of tomatoes, beans or similar, then set it aside for at least 1 hour so the tofu can release any remaining liquid it might be retaining. Drain it again and refrigerate until needed before either frying, baking, marinating or scrambling.

Silken tofu has a much more jelly-like texture and doesn't really stand up to frying or baking (and whatever you do, don't throw it into a stew). It comes into its own when blended, however, making a terrific base for egg-free mayo (see page 172). It is also positively mind-blowing when used in puddings – for proof check out my Chocolate Orange Pots (see page 200).

WHAT'S IN MY PANTRY?

What appears on my shopping list time and time again, I hear you ask? I've been cultivating this selection for years and add to it periodically, but these are pretty much my staples. I've divided the list into handy categories so you can see at a glance what I reach for on a regular basis. As much as I try to buy local, I do frequent supermarkets and the odd health-food store as well.

OILS & BUTTERS

Chilli oil
Coconut oil
Garlic oil
Hazelnut oil
Olive oil (extra-virgin and regular)
Sesame oil (toasted and regular)
Truffle oil
Coconut butter
Dairy-free margarine
Vegetable shortening

GRAINS

Bulgur wheat
Couscous
Freekeh
Millet
Pearl barley
Quinoa (all varieties)
Rice (basmati, brown, risotto and wild)
Spelt

BEANS & LEGUMES

Black beans
Black-eyed peas
Butter beans
Cannellini beans
Chickpeas
Kidney beans
Lentils (green, red, Puy and Beluga)
Yellow split peas

SAUCES, POWDERS, VINEGARS & PASTES

Extracts (vanilla, lemon, orange, coffee and almond)
Mustard (Dijon, wholegrain and English)
Nutritional yeast
Orange blossom water
Rosewater
Sriracha chilli sauce
Tamari and soy sauce
Thai sweet chilli sauce
Chlorella powder
Maca powder
Matcha powder
Raw cacao powder and cocoa
Cider vinegar
Red wine vinegar
Rice mirin
Chipotle paste
Harissa paste
Miso paste (both sweet and dark)
Vegan Thai curry paste (both red and green)

HERBS & SPICES

Bay leaves
Chives
Coriander (fresh)
Dill
Mint
Flat leaf parsley
Rosemary
Tarragon
Thyme
Cardamom pods
Cloves
Dried chilli flakes
Dried oregano
Garam masala
Ground cinnamon
Ground coriander
Ground cumin
Ground turmeric
Kaffir lime leaves
Nutmeg
Peppercorns
Ras el hanout
Salt (fine and coarse sea salt and pink Himalayan)
Smoked paprika
Star anise
Za'atar

NUTS, SEEDS & DRIED FRUITS

Almonds (both flaked and whole)
Brazil nuts
Cashew nuts
Peanuts (unsalted)
Pecan nuts
Pistachios
Walnuts
Chia
Flaxseed
Pumpkin seeds
Sunflower seeds
Dates (medjool)
Dried apricots
Dried berries
Dried mulberries
Raisins

JARRED & CANNED GOODS

Canned tomatoes (plum, chopped, passata and purée)
Coconut cream
Coconut milk
Dairy-free pesto
Nut butters (peanut, almond and cashew)
Sweetcorn
Tahini

FRESH PRODUCE

Apples
Bananas
Lemons and limes
Mangoes
Nectarines
Oranges
Pears
Aubergines
Butternut squash
Chillis
Courgettes
Garlic
Ginger
Kale (including cavolo nero)
Leeks
Mushrooms
Onions
Potatoes (sweet and regular)
Spinach

FOOD FOR FRIENDS

LAID-BACK BRUNCH
....

Brunch is where it's at right now, maybe because the pressure seems to be off earlier in the day or maybe it's because I'm typically more chilled first thing. People generally aren't expecting a gargantuan meal at 11am but I still like to keep them satisfied. My Lemon Chia Pudding is a great way to kick off proceedings because it enlivens the palate and isn't too heavy. Best of all it can be made in advance, which means you can focus on the main event. Because we've started off sweet, I like to graduate to something savoury like my Sweetcorn Fritters, which are surprisingly easy to make and also gluten free. Obviously I'll have a pot of tea or coffee on the go but I also like to fill small tumblers with my Super Green Smoothie. I normally squeeze it through a nut milk bag and refrigerate it before serving, so it's nicely chilled.

> **Lemon Chia Pudding with a Warm Blackberry Compote & Toasted Coconut** (*see* page 38)
> **Sweetcorn Fritters with Quick-pickled Carrot** (*see* page 64)
> **Super Green Smoothie** (*see* page 45)

LIGHT LUNCH
....

I love having friends over for lunch and Romaine Lettuce Wraps are perfect for getting my guests involved – I simply lay everything out on the table and let them help themselves. I pop some Wasabi-dusted Popcorn on the table while I'm prepping, as it's just enough to tide people over until we eat. The Matcha & Lime Pie is so zesty and fresh that most people won't refuse a slice to round off what is a light but satisfying lunch.

> **Wasabi-dusted Popcorn** (*see* page 114)
> **Romaine Lettuce Wraps with Spicy Coconut Chickpeas & Zesty Cauli-rice** (*see* page 54)
> **Matcha & Lime Pie with Macerated Strawberries** (*see* page 192)

INFORMAL DINNER

Informal gatherings are the crux of my social scene. I don't always play host, but when my friends do happen to come over I tend to go all out – without disintegrating into a kitchen-induced meltdown, of course. This Salsa-style Panzanella Salad is the perfect way to start proceedings, because it gets people sharing right off the bat and sets the tone for the evening. The Polenta Pizza is also a bit of a tear and share affair, brilliantly complemented by my absolute new favourite side dish, Crispy Potato Chips with a Parsley & Almond Sauce. Those things will fly off the plate, so you best make a double batch. When it comes to afters, I offer up something savoury for the 'cheese heads' with my Dill-coated Cashew Cheese as well as a refreshing palate cleanser in the form of my Grapefruit, Gin & Sage Granita, both of which can be made in advance, leaving you to enjoy the party. Granted this is more of a summer shindig menu than a cosy winter one, but it's a dinner party that everyone will delight in.

> **Salsa-style Panzanella Salad with Griddled Nectarines** (*see* page 50)
> **Polenta Pizza with Spinach & Roasted Squash** (*see* page 68)
> **Crispy Potato Chips with a Parsley & Almond Sauce** (*see* page 146)
> **Dill-coated Cashew Cheese with Homemade 'Nut-pulp' Crackers** (*see* page 150)
> **Grapefruit, Gin & Sage Granita** (*see* page 210)

WINTER WARMER GATHERING

The festive season brings out the best in us, which is probably why we ramp up the socializing to extra-enthusiastic levels. As much as I love a party, the thought of catering them sometimes makes me break out in a sweat – I often think a halfway house between a formal dinner party and a casual gathering is where I feel most comfortable. This menu reflects my need to know exactly how many I will be feeding while still ensuring the meal is perfectly balanced and, of course, fun! I always like to offer people something to nibble on when they first arrive and this Beluga Lentil & Black Olive Dip works well as an intro. Next up are small warming bowls of Chestnut & Miso Soup served ahead of the main event, which in this case is Celeriac Steaks with a Mushroom Stroganoff Sauce, accompanied by a Massaged Kale & Toasted Walnut Salad. I like to wind things down with a fruit-based dessert like my Mulled Poached Pears – sweet enough to satisfy that nagging sweet tooth but light enough not to overwhelm. Interspersed with glasses of red wine, this menu is a winter warmer to remember.

> **Beluga Lentil & Black Olive Dip** (*see* page 169)
> **Chestnut & Miso Soup with Crunchy Chickpea Croutons** (*see* page 132)
> **Celeriac Steaks with a Mushroom Stroganoff Sauce** (*see* page 166)
> **Massaged Kale & Toasted Walnut Salad with Roasted Celeriac & Persimmon** (*see* page 142)
> **Mulled Poached Pears with a Silky Lemon & Thyme Cashew Cream** (*see* page 202)

ZESTY

CRISPY TOFU SALAD

with a zingy yuzu & miso dressing

SERVES 2

Tofu has a bad reputation, yet while many people think of it as a bland meat imposter, the reality couldn't be further from the truth. Consumed in Asia for centuries, it's a terrific source of protein that absorbs pretty much whatever you throw at it – or, in this particular case, toss it in. Yuzu is a lip-puckeringly sour but fragrant citrus fruit, the juice of which makes for a superb salad dressing. I like to balance out the intense sour notes here with a good dose of smoky sweetness from the maple syrup and some freshness in the form of lime, which helps to make this warm tofu salad something of an unexpected winner.

200g mixed salad leaves
1 carrot, sliced into ribbons
1 courgette, sliced into ribbons
1 persimmon, peeled and sliced
2 tablespoons cornflour
grated zest of 1 lemon
¼ teaspoon sea salt flakes
¼ teaspoon black pepper
250g firm tofu, cut into bite-sized cubes
½ tablespoon groundnut oil
1 teaspoon toasted sesame oil
1 tablespoon poppy seeds

2 spring onions, chopped
lime slices, to garnish

Zingy yuzu & miso dressing
½ tablespoon yuzu juice
½ tablespoon sweet white miso paste
1 thumb-sized piece of fresh root ginger, peeled and minced
juice of ½ lime
1 tablespoon maple syrup

1. To make the dressing, vigorously whisk the ingredients together in a large bowl along with a splash of water to combine. Set aside until needed.

2. Place the salad leaves, carrot and courgette ribbons and persimmon slices in a large bowl.

3. Combine the cornflour with the lemon zest and salt and pepper in a bowl. Add the tofu cubes and toss lightly to coat.

4. Heat the groundnut and sesame oils in a frying pan over a medium–high heat. Add the tofu to the pan and fry for 5–7 minutes, or until golden, tossing the pan from time to time to ensure all sides are crispy.

5. Tip the crispy tofu pieces into the dressing and toss to coat. Add the tofu to the salad bowl and pour over the remaining dressing. Scatter over the poppy seeds and chopped spring onion and garnish with a few slices of lime.

ROASTED BEET, FENNEL & ORANGE SALAD

with a maple & orange dressing

SERVES 4

I often return to this classic combination of ingredients and each time I tweak and update it, I feel like I'm getting closer to the perfect salad. This version is a current favourite and looks especially beautiful when plated up. The roasted oranges almost melt in your mouth and are a great contrast to the fennel and beetroot, which both bring a robust earthiness to proceedings. Of course, no great salad is complete without a dressing and this maple and orange offering is one I perennially covet. This salad is best enjoyed at room temperature, so you can easily make it ahead of time knowing that it's happily marinating in all those wonderful juices, ready to be served.

4 beetroot, peeled and cut into wedges
3 large oranges
2 tablespoons olive oil
2 fennel bulbs, cut into wedges
30g toasted hazelnuts
small handful of dill
sea salt flakes and black pepper

Maple & orange dressing
1 tablespoon Dijon mustard
1 tablespoon cider vinegar
2 tablespoons hazelnut oil
½ tablespoon maple syrup
juice of ½ orange
sea salt flakes and black pepper

1. Preheat the oven to 240°C (220°C fan), Gas Mark 9.

2. Arrange the beetroot wedges on a baking tray, add the grated zest and juice of half an orange and 1 tablespoon of the olive oil, season well and toss to combine. Cover with foil and roast for 40 minutes, then uncover and roast for a further 5–10 minutes, shaking the tray from time to time, until tender. Remove from the oven, season again and squeeze over another 2 tablespoons or so of orange juice.

3. Meanwhile, place the fennel wedges in a baking dish, toss in the rest of the olive oil, season and roast for 25 minutes, shaking the tray occasionally.

4. Cut the peel and rind off the remaining oranges and slice into thick rounds. Add them to the fennel dish and roast for a further 10–15 minutes, or until caramelized.

5. To make the dressing, place all the ingredients in a bowl and whisk vigorously to combine. Season to taste.

6. Arrange the roasted beetroot, fennel and orange pieces on a shallow plate or platter. Drizzle over the maple orange dressing and scatter over the toasted hazelnuts and dill just before serving.

PEA & ROCKET CHICKPEA FLOUR PANCAKE

MAKES 2 LARGE PANCAKES

I was seriously tempted to dub this an 'egg-free omelette', given its ability to replicate that one-time mainstay of my weekly menu so freakishly well. Instead I opted for the somewhat less polarizing title of 'pancake'… although it does produce a very eggy-looking one of these. Vibrant yellow in colour and packed full of peas (and therefore protein), this little number has become something of a personal favourite mainly thanks to its endless versatility. If you'd rather not include the peas in your batter rest assured, it will still be fabulous. Getting this pancake thin might take a bit of practice but it's definitely a skill worth adding to your expanding vegan repertoire.

30g frozen peas
60g gram (chickpea) flour
1 tablespoon flaxseed meal
1 tablespoon nutritional yeast
½ teaspoon baking powder
½ teaspoon ground turmeric
juice of ½ lemon
125ml water
1 heaped tablespoon chopped fresh
　coriander, plus extra to garnish

½ tablespoon coconut oil
70g rocket leaves, plus extra to garnish
sea salt flakes and black pepper

Creamy coconut dressing
4 heaped tablespoons coconut yogurt
grated zest and juice of ½ lemon
1 tablespoon chopped fresh coriander
1 tablespoon chopped mint
sea salt flakes and black pepper

1.　Place the peas in a small bowl and cover with freshly boiled water to defrost.

2.　To make the coconut dressing, whisk the ingredients together in a small bowl until combined. Season to taste and refrigerate until needed.

3.　Sift the gram flour into a mixing bowl. Add the flaxseed meal, yeast, baking powder and turmeric and season with salt and pepper. Whisk to combine.

4.　Make a well in the centre of the flour, add the lemon juice and measured water and whisk to form a batter.

5.　Drain the peas and add to the batter along with the chopped coriander. Stir to combine and set aside for 10 minutes to settle.

6.　Set a crêpe pan or frying pan over a medium heat and brush it with the coconut oil. Ladle in half the batter and, using a spatula, push it to the edges of the pan – you want to get the pancake as thin as possible without it breaking. Cook for 5–7 minutes until the pancake is cooked through (you won't need to flip it).

7.　Add half the rocket and dressing to the centre of the pancake and ease it out on to a plate, using the pan to help gently fold it over. Repeat with the remaining batter. Serve the pancakes garnished with a little extra chopped coriander, rocket and dressing.

SWEET POTATO GRATIN

with a panko lemon crumb

SERVES 4

I dread to think how many sweet potatoes I consume in any given week. Boiled, steamed, roasted or fried, to me they are almost a food group in themselves and one that I never tire of experimenting with. This easy gratin dish might sound indulgent but it's actually a pretty healthy alternative to its dairy-laden counterpart and the flaky, Japanese-style panko breadcrumbs make for a deliciously crunchy topping. A dauphinoise in essence, it's always sure to impress – whether you're hosting a formal dinner party or creating a casual lunch scenario. In my opinion it works for any food-centred occasion and is yet another string to add to your sweet potato-loving bow.

1 teaspoon coconut oil
2 large sweet potatoes, peeled, halved and
    sliced into 1cm thick pieces
4 teaspoons za'atar
300ml soy cream (or oat cream or coconut
    milk)
50g panko breadcrumbs
grated zest of 1 lemon
sea salt flakes and black pepper

1. Preheat the oven to 220°C (200°C fan), Gas Mark 7. Grease a 30 x 20cm ovenproof dish with the coconut oil.

2. Arrange the sweet potato pieces in the prepared dish in an even overlapping layer until the base is completely covered. Season with salt and pepper and sprinkle over 1 teaspoon of the za'atar, then pour over 100ml of the soy cream. Repeat the layers in the same fashion twice more for a total of 3 layers, ensuring all the sweet potato has been used and being sure to reserve 1 teaspoon of the za'atar.

3. Cover the gratin with lightly greased foil and bake for 50 minutes.

4. Meanwhile, combine the breadcrumbs, lemon zest and remaining za'atar in a bowl and season generously with salt and pepper.

5. Sprinkle the breadcrumb mix over the gratin and bake for a further 15–20 minutes until golden. Serve immediately.

CRISPY CINNAMON POTATO TACOS

with a lime & jalapeño soured cream

SERVES 4–6

There are few things in life that give me more pleasure than tacos. With endless filling possibilities, wrapped in either crispy or soft tortillas (both have their virtues), they are the food equivalent of 'one-size-fits-all'. I've never met a person who doesn't relish wrapping their lips around one and if I ever did, I'm fairly certain we would not get along. If you're seeking a fail-safe dinner party hit then these crispy cinnamon tatties – my current favourite taco incarnation – are most likely it, though I guarantee most questions will be about the lime and jalapeño soured cream, which is borderline life-changing.

750g salad potatoes, halved lengthways and
   cut into 5mm thick slices
1½ teaspoons ground cinnamon, plus extra
   to serve
½ teaspoon cumin seeds
¼ teaspoon ground coriander
1 tablespoon maple syrup
3 tablespoons olive or rapeseed oil
large handful of fresh coriander, roughly
   chopped
grated zest of 1 lime
sea salt flakes and black pepper

Lime & jalapeño soured cream
150g cashews, soaked and drained (*see* page 8)
100ml water
grated zest and juice of 1 lime
1 teaspoon cider vinegar

1 tablespoon pickled jalapeños
sea salt flakes and black pepper

Sweetcorn & radish salsa
100g sweetcorn kernels, preferably raw
4 radishes, finely chopped
1 celery stick, finely chopped
2 spring onions, finely chopped
1 green chilli, finely chopped
grated zest and juice of 1 lime
1 tablespoon roughly chopped flat leaf parsley
1 tablespoon roughly chopped dill
sea salt flakes and black pepper

To serve
10–12 taco-sized tortillas
200g rocket leaves
lime juice

1. Preheat the oven to 220°C (200°C fan), Gas Mark 7.
2. To make the soured cream, place the cashews in a blender with the measured water, lime juice, vinegar and jalapeños. Season and blend for at least 10 minutes, or until completely smooth. Scrape down the sides with a spatula every few minutes, bearing in mind that the cream will go through several stages until you achieve the desired smooth consistency. Transfer to a bowl and refrigerate until needed.
3. Place the potatoes in an ovenproof dish and sprinkle over the cinnamon, cumin and coriander, then drizzle with the maple syrup and 2 tablespoons of the oil. Season generously and toss to combine. Roast in the oven for 35–40 minutes, or until golden and crisp, shaking the pan from time to time. Remove from the oven, season and toss through the chopped coriander and lime zest.

4. To make the salsa, place the sweetcorn kernels in a large bowl with the chopped radish, celery, spring onion and chilli. Add the lime zest and juice, season generously and stir to combine. Add the parsley and dill, stir and set aside until needed.

5. Heat the tortillas on a lightly oiled griddle pan and keep warm in a clean tea towel.

6. Spread each tortilla with a light smear of soured cream, then top with some rocket leaves. followed by crispy potatoes, sweetcorn salsa and some more soured cream. Finish with a squeeze of lime juice, dust with cinnamon and serve.

ANGEL HAIR PASTA

with a lemon, dill & walnut sauce

SERVES 4

Pasta. Unsurprisingly, I have a major soft spot for the stuff – it's the carb that just keeps on giving and I am endlessly amazed at my ability to never tire of it. My mother often reminds me of my early obsession with ravioli, so this love affair clearly has deep roots. And while this gorgeously simple walnut sauce is probably not something my six-year-old self would have appreciated, this thirty-six year old version is borderline fanatical about it. Perhaps that's because it can made in mere minutes (we're talking ten, maximum) or maybe it's because a stripped-back pasta dish is all we need to fill that midweek comfort food hole. I affectionately refer to this recipe as 'restoration in a bowl' and strongly recommend you earmark this page for I'm-in-a-rush-but-still-want-something-fabulous moments.

1 small garlic clove
grated zest and juice of 1 lemon
small bunch of dill, plus extra to garnish
1 teaspoon Dijon mustard
1 teaspoon capers
3 tablespoons extra virgin olive oil
70g walnuts
300g angel hair spaghetti
sea salt flakes and black pepper

1. Place the garlic, lemon zest and juice, dill, mustard, capers and olive oil in a small blender or processor. Season generously and blitz briefly to combine, then add the walnuts and blitz again to form a coarse pesto-like sauce.

2. Bring a large pan of salted water to the boil. Add the pasta and cook for 2–3 minutes, or just under the recommended cooking time. Drain the pasta, reserving 100ml of the cooking water.

3. Return the pasta to the pan, season generously and add the walnut sauce along with the reserved cooking water. Gently combine over a low heat until all the strands are coated, then divide between bowls and serve garnished with a little extra dill.

ZA'ATAR ROASTED VEGETABLE PLATTER

with a carrot pesto & basil oil drizzle

SERVES 4

I have a thing about platters. I love having food arranged and displayed in such a way that makes it seem tactile and exciting. Roasted vegetables lend themselves particularly well to this method of serving, especially when paired with a chunky carrot pesto. Since I discovered carrot pesto a little while back, it's quickly overtaken all other varieties in my kitchen. Not only does it make for a great dressing but I also use it as a dip or sandwich spread and of course it's wonderful stirred through pasta too.

1 head of cauliflower, broken into large florets
1 head of broccoli, broken into large florets
2 large courgettes, cut diagonally into 1cm
  pieces
1 tablespoon olive oil
grated zest of 1 lemon, plus juice of ½ lemon
1 heaped teaspoon za'atar
sea salt flakes and black pepper

Carrot pesto
250g roughly chopped carrots
75g pine nuts
1 tablespoon cider vinegar
juice of ½ lemon
50ml extra virgin olive oil
sea salt flakes and black pepper

Basil oil drizzle
large bunch of basil
¼ teaspoon sea salt flakes
¼ teaspoon black pepper
juice of ½ lemon
50ml extra virgin olive oil

1. Preheat the oven to 220°C (200°C fan), Gas Mark 7.
2. To make the carrot pesto, place the carrots in a food processor and pulse to break them into fine chunks. Add the pine nuts, vinegar and lemon juice, season and blitz for a few seconds before gradually pouring in the olive oil and continuing to bliz until the pesto is thick and creamy. Refrigerate until needed.
3. Arrange the vegetables on a baking sheet and pour over the olive oil and lemon juice. Add the za'atar and lemon zest and season generously. Toss to combine and roast for 35–40 minutes, turning the vegetables occasionally to ensure they roast evenly.
4. Transfer the roasted vegetables to a serving platter and generously adorn with the carrot pesto.
5. For the basil oil drizzle, place the basil leaves in a pestle and mortar with the salt and pepper and muddle until it forms a paste. Add the lemon juice and olive oil and vigorously combine. Season to taste, then drizzle over the roasted vegetables and serve.

SEASONED CAULIFLOWER

with a savoury citrus sauce

SERVES 6

Cauliflower is my meat. This might seem like a strange thing to say but it really does fill that dreaded hole on the plate; not least because of its fibrous qualities but also because it soaks up any marinade so well – all those nooks and crannies cry out for a suitably robust sauce and make it a terrific backdrop for most flavours. I often use this orange sauce with parsley and pistachios because it pairs beautifully with the cauliflower's delicate flavour. This dish makes a great simple starter, though it can also be served alongside an array of salads and sides for a more substantial meal that will be sure to wow.

1 head of cauliflower, outer leaves removed and cut into six equal-sized wedges

Marinade
1 tablespoon Dijon mustard
½ tablespoon maple syrup
½ tablespoon olive oil
grated zest and juice of ½ orange
¼ teaspoon sea salt flakes
pinch of white pepper

Savoury citrus sauce
60g flat leaf parsley
1 spring onion
4 tablespoons toasted pistachios
grated zest and juice of ½ orange
1 green chilli
2 tablespoons extra virgin olive oil
sea salt flakes and black pepper

To serve
30g slivered pistachios
small handful of torn flat leaf parsley
grated zest of ½ orange

1. Preheat the oven to 240°C (220°C fan), Gas Mark 9.
2. Whisk the marinade ingredients together in a small bowl. Generously brush the cauliflower wedges with the marinade, reserving a little for cooking.
3. Transfer the cauliflower wedges to a baking tray and roast for 25–30 minutes, turning once and brushing with the reserved marinade, until browned.
4. Meanwhile, place all the sauce ingredients in a food processor and blend to combine (or pound the ingredients together using a pestle and mortar for a more rustic option).
5. To serve, dollop a generous spoonful of the sauce on to the centre of 6 individual small serving plates and place a cauliflower wedge on top of each. Scatter over a few slivered pistachios, a little torn parsley and some orange zest just before serving.

HOT LEMONY ARTICHOKE & SPINACH DIP

SERVES 4

I love a good dip and this one is a nice departure from the usual hummus on offer at parties. Its zesty notes are offset brilliantly by its unctuous creaminess, the result of a terrific cashew–tofu combo that sounds odd but totally works! Don't worry if you can only get your hands on antipasti-style jarred artichokes, simply rinse off any excess oil and herbs before using. Likewise, the nutritional yeast is not crucial; it adds a certain 'cheesiness' that some people adore but it's not the deciding factor in the success of this simple but lovely little dish.

200g cashew nuts, soaked and drained
(*see* page 8)
150ml water
½ teaspoon sea salt flakes
½ teaspoon black pepper
grated zest and juice of 1 lemon

150g silken tofu
3 tablespoons nutritional yeast (optional)
½ tablespoon Dijon mustard
½ tablespoon olive oil
150g baby leaf spinach
150g pre-cooked artichokes

1. Preheat the oven to 240°C (220°C fan), Gas Mark 9.
2. Place the cashew nuts in a blender with the measured water, salt, pepper and half the lemon juice. Blend until smooth before adding the tofu, yeast (if using) and mustard. Season and blend on a high speed for 5–7 minutes until completely smooth and pourable, scraping down the sides from time to time as you go.
3. Heat the olive oil in a pan over a low–medium heat, add the spinach and cook for 1–2 minutes, or until gently wilted. Transfer to a blender together with the artichokes and lemon zest, season and pulse to combine. Pour in 250ml of the cashew and tofu cream and the remaining lemon juice, season generously and pulse until the mixture just comes together but still retains some texture.
4. Transfer to a baking dish and bake for 20 minutes until browned, then remove from the oven and leave to cool for a few minutes before serving. It's great with crudités.

OAT & ORANGE BLOSSOM 'SHROVE TUESDAY' PANCAKES

with chocolate sauce

MAKES 5

Almost crêpe-thin, these oaty pancakes are a nod to the ones I used to enjoy on Shrove Tuesday with my family. The key to getting them as thin as possible is transferring the batter to a jug and practising the 'pour and swirl' – pouring the batter into the preheated pan and gently tipping the pan from side to side (in a sort of circular motion) until the batter meets the edges. And while these pancakes are wonderful served simply with a squeeze of lime and a drizzle of agave nectar, I've gone down the chocolate sauce route here for a bit of well-deserved indulgence. Pancake Day never tasted so good!

150g rolled oats
½ teaspoon bicarbonate of soda
pinch of sea salt flakes
200ml almond milk
juice of ½ orange
½ tablespoon orange blossom water
½ tablespoon agave nectar
100ml water, plus extra if necessary
1–2 tablespoons coconut oil

oat flakes, to decorate

Chocolate sauce
1 heaped tablespoon coconut oil
2 heaped tablespoons raw cacao powder or cocoa
1 tablespoon agave nectar
pinch of sea salt flakes

1. Place the oats in a small food processor or blender and blitz to a fine flour. Transfer to a mixing bowl along with the bicarbonate of soda and salt and stir to combine.

2. Whisk the almond milk, orange juice, orange blossom water and agave nectar together in a separate bowl.

3. Make a well in the centre of the flour and pour in the almond milk mixture together with the measured water and whisk to combine. The batter should be the consistency of single cream and tends to thicken over time, so thin it out with a little extra water as necessary. Transfer to a jug.

4. Heat 1 teaspoon of coconut oil in a nonstick frying pan over a medium–high heat. Pour in just enough batter to coat the bottom, swirling to ensure it reaches the edges. Cook for at least 5 minutes, or until bubbles form and the edges appeared cooked – the pancakes can be delicate, so be sure not to flip them too soon. Flip the pancake (or turn carefully with a wide spatula) then cook for a further 3–5 minutes until thoroughly cooked. Transfer to a warmed plate and cover with a clean tea towel. Repeat until all the batter is used, adding an extra teaspoon of coconut oil to the pan between pancakes.

5. To make the chocolate sauce, heat the coconut oil in a saucepan until melted. Take it off the heat and whisk in the cacao powder, agave nectar and salt until smooth and glossy. Pour into a small jug.

6. Fold the pancakes and arrange them on a large plate or platter. Pour over the chocolate sauce and sprinkle over a few oat flakes just before serving.

LEMON CHIA PUDDING

with a warm blackberry compote & toasted coconut

SERVES 2

Chia crops up regularly in my cooking. Those unassuming seeds that transform into tapioca-like pearls once they meet liquid have long held my fascination – not only because of their nutritional properties but also because they satisfy me until lunch. And while I try not to get too hung up on their 'healthy' credentials, it's difficult to ignore the impressive benefits that range from their high fibre and protein content through to the essential omega-3 fatty acids they contain – though let's be honest, none of that truly matters if they're not up to scratch in the taste department. I like to bolster their neutral (some might say 'non-existent') flavour with a dash of citrus. The addition of lemon in this recipe really livens up breakfast time and also makes for an excellent brunch intro, especially when paired with this comforting warm blackberry compote. Like rice pud and jam. Only better.

250ml oat milk (*see* page 9),
    plus extra if necessary
3 tablespoons canned coconut cream
grated zest and juice of 1 small lemon or lime
pinch of pink Himalayan salt
3 tablespoons maple syrup
4 tablespoons chia seeds

Blackberry compote
150g fresh blackberries
1 tablespoon maple syrup
juice of ½ orange

To serve
finely sliced orange peel
2 heaped tablespoons toasted coconut flakes

1. Whisk the oat milk, coconut cream, lemon zest and juice, salt and syrup together in a bowl until combined. Stir through the chia seeds and refrigerate for at least an hour, preferably overnight.

2. To make the blackberry compote, bring the ingredients to a gentle simmer in a small saucepan and cook for 10–15 minutes until thick and syrupy. Lightly mash the berries, leaving a few whole, and set aside until needed.

3. Remove the pudding from the refrigerator and stir to loosen the mixture, adding a touch more oat milk if it is looking a little stiff.

4. Divide the pudding among shallow bowls, topping each with a large spoonful of the compote, some finely sliced orange peel and a smattering of toasted coconut.

HOMEMADE CASHEW YOGURT

with griddled grapefruit

SERVES 2

Making your own yogurt can feel slightly overwhelming, particularly if you're unfamiliar with probiotics. Luckily this 'cashew-gurt' is as straightforward as it gets, mainly because you have complete control over the texture and thickness without having to resort to tapioca starch or agar agar. I like my yogurt quite thick and unctuous, but if you prefer it thinner simply add more water. Delicately flavoured with vanilla and lemon, this is a firm breakfast favourite.

200g cashew nuts
juice of ½ lemon
2–3 tablespoons maple syrup or other vegan sweetener
vanilla pod, seeds scraped
pinch of Himalayan salt
175–225ml water
3 probiotic capsules

Griddled grapefruit
½ tablespoon pomegranate molasses
2 tablespoons palm sugar
juice of ½ grapefruit
1 large grapefruit, peeled and cut into rounds

1. To make the yogurt, place the cashew nuts in a bowl, cover with water and leave to soak for 8–12 hours.

2. Drain and rinse the cashew nuts, then place in a blender with the lemon juice, maple syrup, vanilla seeds, salt and water (175ml for a thick yoghurt and up to 225ml for a lighter variety). Blend until completely smooth, scraping down the sides periodically.

3. Transfer the cashew nut mixture to a scrupulously clean bowl or jar and add the contents of the probiotic capsules. Whisk, cover with a clean tea towel or muslin cloth and set aside in a dark, dry place for up to 24 hours – or 48 hours for a more potent yoghurt.

4. Once its fermented, refrigerate the yogurt until needed. It's best served chilled and will keep for up to a week.

5. To make the griddled grapefruit, whisk the pomegranate molasses, palm sugar and grapefruit juice together until smooth. Heat a griddle pan over a medium–high heat, add the grapefruit pieces and cook until charred on both sides. Transfer the griddled grapefruit to the bowl and leave to marinate for 30 minutes. Arrange the grapefruit slices on a plate and serve with a spoonful of cashew yogurt.

CLEMENTINE & COCONUT LASSI

with a touch of pink Himalayan salt

SERVES 2

My biggest regret about visiting India almost a decade ago was not consuming more lassi while I was there. Not yet vegan at the time, this was my first proper foray into vegetarian food and it really opened my eyes. Traditional lassi contains dairy, of course, but I think coconut yogurt is an even better way of enjoying this satisfyingly exotic little drink. The addition of salt is crucial and sets this lassi apart from a regular smoothie – balancing the sweet and slightly sour flavours. I prefer to drink it chilled and poured into glasses filled with ice – a creamy, moreish concoction to be sipped and savoured.

150g coconut yogurt
juice of 2 clementines
½ ripe mango
300ml chilled coconut water
1 tablespoon agave nectar
pinch of pink Himalayan salt

To serve
pink Himalayan salt
ground coriander
torn basil leaves

1. Place all the ingredients into a high-speed blender and blitz until completely combined.
2. Divide between glasses, sprinkle over a touch of salt and a dusting of ground coriander along with some torn fresh basil. Enjoy immediately or chill in the refrigerator for up to a day until needed.

FRESH

SMOOTHIE 101

Smoothies have fast become a regular morning feature in my life. Aside from being incredibly delicious and quick to make, they are also a great way to inject those much-talked-about five servings of fruit and veg into your day…or should that be ten now? I can never keep up. Because I rarely have the same fruit in my bowl or veg in my refrigerator I've developed a little strategy for getting the most out of (and into) my smoothies with whatever I happen to have in my kitchen. If you're anything like me you're bound to have a least one item from each list to hand, making it super-easy to create the most balanced smoothie bowl.

LIQUID

plant milk (soy, oat, almond, coconut or other)

juice (such as orange, grapefruit, apple, lemon or lime)

coconut water

filtered water

GREENS

kale

spinach

cavolo nero

romaine lettuce

broccoli stalks

parsley

mint

celery

peas

FRUIT

banana (frozen or fresh)

apple

pear

pineapple

melon

mango

nectarine or peach

berries (frozen or fresh)

OTHER

nut butter (such as peanut, almond, cashew or hazelnut)

dairy-free yogurt (such as soy, coconut or almond)

avocado

soaked nuts (cashew nuts, almonds etc.)

rolled oats

seeds (such as chia, hemp or flaxseed)

fresh root ginger or turmeric

spices and powders (such as cinnamon, cacao, maca, spirulina, chlorella or acai)

1. Place your chosen liquid in the bottom of a blender, add the remaining ingredients and blitz until completely smooth.
2. Transfer to a bowl, add your choice of toppings and serve.

Here are three combinations I currently have on rotation – simply follow the method on the opposite page. Strangely enough, none of these smoothies contain banana.

NECTARINE & OATS

Top with raspberries, sliced nectarine and poppy seeds. Make this ahead of time and let it chill overnight for a super-quick, nutritious breakfast.

2 ripe nectarines or peaches
50g raspberries
2 medjool dates, pitted
50g rolled oats
20g flaked almonds or 1 heaped teaspoon
    almond butter

¼ teaspoon vanilla powder (or seeds from
    ½ vanilla pod)
100ml oat or almond milk
3 heaped tablespoons coconut or soy yogurt
juice of ½ lemon

ULTIMATE 'NO BANANA' BERRY BOWL

Serve this parfait-style with homemade rawnola (*see* page 46) and a handful of frozen berries. For it to taste at its best, this must be eaten immediately.

150g frozen mixed berries
1 celery stick
50ml rice milk
50ml orange juice

3 heaped tablespoons soy or other dairy-free
    yogurt
1 heaped tablespoon cashew butter
2 heaped tablespoons milled flaxseed
1 tablespoon maple syrup

SUPER GREEN SMOOTHIE

For a glorious, pulp-free green juice add slightly more water at the blending stage and strain it through a nut milk bag or muslin cloth before serving. This smoothie refrigerates well.

200ml filtered or coconut water
150g fresh pineapple
1 apple
1 thumb-sized piece of fresh root ginger, peeled

50g spinach
50g kale
juice of ½ grapefruit

DATE & COCONUT RAWNOLA

MAKES 6 SERVINGS

My love for granola really knows no bounds and I'm always looking for new and interesting ways to tweak how I make it. It didn't occur to me until relatively recently that the raw mixture itself – almost like cookie dough – is really rather wonderful, so why bake it at all? The crucial point here is texture, so go easy on the blending; once the mixture reaches the 'sticky rubble' stage it's time to stop or else you begin to enter bliss-ball territory (not necessarily a bad thing, but not what we're after here). I like to reserve half the coconut for a quick pulse towards the end so you're left with lots of lovely flakes but feel free to add it all at once or play around by varying the nuts and dried fruit – I'm thinking an apricot and pistachio combo would be spectacular.

100g rolled oats
50g almonds
100g coconut flakes
4 medjool dates, pitted

50g raisins
1 teaspoon ground cinnamon
¼ teaspoon sea salt flakes

1. Place the oats, almonds and half the coconut flakes in a food processor and pulse briefly to break down.
2. Add the dates, raisins, cinnamon and salt and blitz for 1–2 minutes to form a sticky rubble – the mix will appear dry initially but will eventually form sticky clusters (be careful not to overwork it). Add the remaining coconut flakes and pulse to combine.
3. Transfer the rawnola to a clean jar and store in a cool place or the refrigerator – it will keep for up to 10 days.
4. Serve with your favourite dairy-free yogurt, with plant milk and fresh fruit, or on its own as a snack.

CARROT, CUCUMBER & APPLE SALAD

with a ginger & passionfruit dressing

SERVES 2-4

Sometimes I like to return to familiar ingredients in a bid to find new and exciting ways to make them shine. I always have an apple, carrots and cucumber to hand, which makes this simple salad a bit of a go-to recipe of mine. I've resisted the temptation to add a smattering of seeds here (although sunflower and pumpkin seeds would work particularly well), instead letting the glorious ginger dressing take centre stage – it really is that good! For something so simple, this salad has the ability to be a real talking point when arranged on a platter and garnished with what is perhaps my favourite mix of herbs. As the Barefoot Contessa would say, it's carrot salad 'with the volume turned up'…right up.

1 large carrot, peeled and cut into matchsticks

½ cucumber, halved lengthways, seeds removed and cut into half-moons

1 celery stick, finely chopped

1 heaped tablespoon roughly chopped dill

1 heaped tablespoon roughly chopped fresh coriander

1 heaped tablespoon roughly chopped mint

1 large apple, peeled, cored and sliced

Ginger & passionfruit dressing

1 thumb-sized piece of fresh root ginger, peeled and finely grated

1 heaped teaspoon Dijon mustard

juice of ½ lemon

½ tablespoon cider vinegar

½ tablespoon agave nectar

1 passionfruit, seeds strained

3 tablespoons extra virgin olive oil

sea salt flakes and black pepper

1. Put the carrot, cucumber and celery pieces in a large bowl.
2. To make the dressing, add all the ingredients to a separate bowl, season generously and whisk together vigorously until emulsified.
3. Pour two-thirds of the dressing over the salad and, using your hands, toss gently to combine.
4. Add the chopped herbs to the bowl, reserving a small handful for garnish. Gently toss to ensure they are evenly dispersed, then pile the salad on to a large platter or plate and arrange the apple slices in and around it.
5. Pour over the remaining dressing and scatter over the rest of the herbs to finish.

SALSA-STYLE PANZANELLA SALAD

with griddled nectarines

SERVES 2–4

This dish epitomizes summer for me. A gorgeously vibrant salsa interspersed with crisp griddled tortilla chips and sweet charred nectarines, it is a stunning sharing plate – perfect for a relaxed girls' night in. For me, the ideal salsa lies in the 'chop'; I am fastidious about keeping each individual ingredient perfectly proportioned, guaranteeing the ultimate bite each and every time. I like to use the crisp edge of the tortilla to cut through the soft nectarine before scooping up the salsa, ensuring maximum eating pleasure.

2 large flour tortillas
50ml olive oil
2 ripe nectarines, halved, pitted and cut
   into thick slices
3 tomatoes, diced
1 large ripe avocado, diced
1 small green chilli, minced
1 shallot, finely chopped
juice of ½ lime
small bunch off flat leaf parsley,
   roughly chopped
sea salt flakes and black pepper

Dressing
1 ripe nectarine, pitted
juice of 1 lime
1 heaped teaspoon palm sugar
1 heaped teaspoon pomegranate molasses
sea salt flakes and black pepper

1. Heat a griddle pan over a medium–high heat. Lightly brush the tortillas with the olive oil and cut into large triangles. Griddle the tortillas for 3–4 minutes on each side until crispy and charred, then remove from the pan.

2. Add the nectarine slices to the griddle pan and cook for 1–2 minutes on each side until lightly charred.

3. Put the tomatoes, avocado, chilli and shallot in a mixing bowl, squeeze over the lime juice and season generously with salt and pepper. Stir through the parsley, reserving a little for garnish.

4. To make the dressing, place all the ingredients in a blender, season and blitz together to form a smooth purée.

5. Pile the salsa into the centre of a shallow bowl or dish and arrange the tortillas and griddled nectarine around it. Drizzle over the dressing, garnish with the remaining parsley and serve.

CAULI-RICE MAKI ROLLS

with beetroot & apple

SERVES 2-4

I am often put off making sushi mainly because I can rarely be bothered to boil, cool and season the rice but since swapping to cauli-rice it's become much more of a regular feature on my menu. The fillings vary, although recently I've been quite taken with this beetroot and apple pairing – having that sweet crunch in there truly makes all the difference. Cauli-rice in itself isn't terribly exciting but adding a little lemon zest, chilli and herbs like this suddenly transforms it into something quite special.

4–8 nori seaweed sheets
small handful of watercress or pea shoots
2 small cooked beetroot, cut lengthways into
thin strips
½ cucumber, cut into matchsticks
1 apple, peeled, cored and cut into
matchsticks

Cauli-rice
1 small head of cauliflower, broken into
florets
½ green chilli

1 thumb-sized piece of fresh root ginger,
peeled
small handful of flat leaf parsley
small handful of fresh mint
grated zest of 1 lemon
sea salt flakes and black pepper

Dipping sauce
3 heaped tablespoons egg-free mayo
1 heaped tablespoon Thai sweet chilli sauce
juice of ½ lemon

1. To make the cauli-rice, add the cauliflower florets to a food processor with the rest of the ingredients, season generously and pulse together to form a nubbly, coarse 'rice'.

2. For the dipping sauce, put the ingredients in a small bowl and mix together well. Set aside.

3. Lay a nori sheet on a sushi rolling mat, shiny-side down, and cover three-quarters of the sheet with the cauli-rice, leaving a gap at the end furthest away from you.

4. Beginning with the watercress and following with the beetroot, cucumber and then the apple, layer the ingredients in a horizontal line across the middle of the sheet. Begin to roll the nori sheet up away from you, tucking it tightly as you go and dabbing the gap at the end with a little water to seal. Repeat with the remaining nori sheets and filling ingredients.

5. Fill a large jug with water and use it to wet a sharp knife. Shake any excess water of the knife before slicing the sushi rolls into equal-sized rounds. Transfer to a platter and serve with the dipping sauce.

ROMAINE LETTUCE WRAPS

with spicy coconut chickpeas & zesty cauli-rice

SERVES 2

Goodness, these are good. I know that lettuce wraps reek of dullness but these are too tasty to be ignored. I recommend getting the biggest, most badass romaine you can find – lacklustre leaves really won't do here. It's also crucial to let the chickpeas cool slightly before assembling the wraps, otherwise you might have end up with a droop situation on your hands.

1 head of romaine lettuce, leaves separated

Zesty cauli-rice
1 small head of cauliflower, broken into florets
large bunch of fresh coriander
2 spring onions
grated zest and juice of ½ large lemon
1 heaped teaspoon ground cumin
½ teaspoon sea salt flakes
30g toasted flaked almonds
30g raisins or chopped apricots
black pepper

Spicy coconut chickpeas
1 heaped teaspoon coconut oil
2 shallots, finely sliced

230g canned chickpeas, rinsed and drained
1 teaspoon smoked paprika
1 heaped teaspoon tomato purée
8 cherry tomatoes, halved
125ml canned coconut milk
1 teaspoon sambal olek (or other chilli paste)
1 heaped tablespoon finely chopped fresh coriander, plus extra to serve
sea salt flakes and black pepper

Avocado & dill crema
1 ripe avocado
juice of ½ lemon
40ml canned coconut milk
small handful of dill, finely chopped
sea salt flakes and black pepper

1.   To make the cauli-rice, add the cauliflower florets to a food processor with the coriander, spring onions, lemon zest, cumin and salt. Pulse together to form a nubbly, coarse 'rice', then transfer to a large bowl. Add the flaked almonds, raisins and lemon juice and stir to combine. Check for seasoning, stir and set aside until needed.

2.   For the spicy coconut chickpeas, heat the coconut oil in a small frying pan over a medium heat, add the shallots and sauté for 3–4 minutes until translucent. Add the chickpeas and smoked paprika, lightly season with salt and pepper and sauté for 1–2 minutes, then stir in the tomato purée and cherry tomatoes. Pour over the coconut milk and a splash of water, bring to a simmer and cook, covered with a lid, for 10 minutes, or until the tomatoes have begun to soften.

3.   Stir through the sambal olek and continue to simmer for 3–4 minutes until the sauce has thickened and reduced. Stir through the coriander, then remove from the heat and leave for 5 minutes to cool (you want to serve this warm not piping hot).

4. Meanwhile, make the crema by mashing the avocado in a bowl with a fork until smooth. Add the lemon juice, coconut milk and dill, season generously and mix together until thick and creamy.

5. To assemble the wraps, spread the lettuce leaves first with the crema, then layer over a generous amount of cauli-rice and top with a spoonful of the warm chickpeas. Scatter over a final smattering of coriander to finish.

BACK-TO-FRONT BIBIMBAP BOWL

SERVES 2

I've flipped the typical bibimbap on its head here, using a cold (raw) broccoli rice base and keeping the hot element for the toppings. Many such bowls typically contain some egg component so I've included my ultimate tofu scramble here, which is my plant-based attempt to replicate that same eggy texture – it's surprisingly convincing. To make this four-part bowl a touch more straightforward and help minimize the kitchen mess, I use the same pan for each element, wiping it clean each time in between. In true bibimbap style, of course, don't forget to give it all a good mix before digging in!

Broccoli rice
1 small head of broccoli, broken into florets
    and stalk reserved
small bunch of flat leaf parsley
grated zest of 1 lemon
sea salt flakes and black pepper

Spinach
1 teaspoon coconut oil
300g spinach
1 tablespoon tamari or soy sauce
1 tablespoon rice mirin
squeeze of lemon juice
1 tablespoon sesame seeds

Carrot
1 garlic clove
1 thumb-sized piece of fresh root ginger,
    peeled
2 tablespoons toasted sesame oil
1 tablespoon tamari
1 teaspoon cider vinegar

juice of ½ lemon
1 teaspoon palm sugar
1 teaspoon coconut oil
2 large carrots, cut into ribbons

Scrambled tofu
1 teaspoon coconut oil
1 small onion, halved lengthways and sliced
    into half-moons
300g firm tofu, crumbled
1 heaped teaspoon ground turmeric
2 tablespoons tamari
1 teaspoon dried chilli flakes
juice of ½ lemon
50ml soy milk (or other plant milk,
    see **page 9)**
1 large tomato, diced

To serve
freshly chopped flat leaf parsley
Sriracha or other chilli sauce
cucumber slices

1. To make the broccoli rice, add the broccoli florets and stalk to a food processor together with the parsley and lemon zest. Season generously and pulse together to form a nubbly, coarse 'rice'. Set aside until needed.

2. For the spinach, melt the coconut oil in a frying pan over a medium heat, add the spinach, tamari, rice mirin and lemon juice and cook until wilted. Add the sesame seeds, toss to combine and transfer to a warm oven.

3. For the carrot, whisk all the ingredients except the coconut oil and carrot ribbons together in an ovenproof bowl to form a dressing. Wipe the pan clean with kitchen paper, then add the coconut oil and carrot ribbons and cook over a medium heat for 3–4 minutes until tender. Add the carrot to the bowl with the dressing and toss to combine, then transfer to the oven to keep warm.

4. To make the scrambled tofu, wipe the pan clean with kitchen paper again, then add the coconut oil and onion, season and cook for 3–4 minutes over a medium heat until the onion begins to soften. Stir in the tofu and turmeric and season generously, then add the tamari, chilli flakes, lemon juice and soy milk and cook for 10 minutes, or until the tofu is cooked through. Add the tomato, season again and sauté for a further 5 minutes. Remove from the heat.

5. To serve, divide the broccoli rice among two bowls and top with the wilted spinach, dressed carrot ribbons and scrambled tofu. Garnish with freshly chopped parsley, lashings of hot sauce (I recommend Sriracha) and freshly sliced cucumber.

GLASS NOODLE SALAD

SERVES 2-4

Rice noodles are a godsend. If ever I'm pushed for time or haven't the energy to cook properly, these are what I wheel out – I call it a 'shortcut with style'. While these are perfectly wonderful eaten alone, I also often serve them as part of a larger meal or buffet so people can wrangle with the noodles themselves and enjoy their clean-tasting, Asian-inspired vibe. They also happen to look rather pretty, especially adorned with a scattering of black sesame seeds to set off the glorious, pale green hue. Grab your chopsticks and let's go.

2 rice noodle nests
100g frozen edamame
½ cucumber, cut into ribbons
100g sugar snap peas, sliced diagonally

Zesty Asian dressing
1 small red chilli, finely chopped
1 thumb-sized piece of fresh root ginger,
**   peeled and grated**

grated zest and juice of 1 lime
2 tablespoons tamari
½ tablespoon sesame oil
1½ tablespoons maple syrup
½ tablespoon rice mirin

To serve
2 spring onions, sliced
2 tablespoons black sesame seeds

1. Place the rice noodles and edamame in a large bowl and cover with freshly boiled water. Leave to soak for 8–10 minutes, stirring occasionally with chopsticks to break up the nests of noodles. When the noodles are soft, drain and set aside.

2. To make the dressing, mix the chilli and ginger together in a small bowl to form a paste, then add the remaining ingredients and whisk together vigorously.

3. Pour the dressing over the noodles and combine, using your hands. Add the cucumber and sugar snap peas to the bowl and mix to combine. Refrigerate until needed.

4. When ready to serve, garnish with the spring onion and sesame seeds.

WATERMELON, WATERCRESS & CUCUMBER SALAD

SERVES 4

Nothing says summer like a watermelon salad. Tossed with ribbons of fresh cucumber and doused in a creamy tahini sauce, this is one seriously beautiful bowl that is almost (almost) too beautiful to eat. This salad might be simple but it packs a punch – full of fresh flavours and contrasting textures, it never fails to impress.

75g watercress
1 small watermelon (about 750g), rind
    removed and cut into thick triangular
    wedges
1 small cucumber, cut into ribbons
1 celery stick, finely sliced

1 spring onion, finely sliced
1 heaped tablespoon chopped mint
30g pumpkin seeds
1 x 'Goes-with-Everything' Tahini Sauce
   (see page 151)

1. Cover a large plate or serving platter with the watercress, then layer over the watermelon wedges and top with the cucumber, celery and spring onion.
2. To make the tahini dressing, put all the ingredients in a bowl and whisk to combine. Taste and adjust the seasoning.
3. Drizzle a few tablespoons of the tahini sauce over the salad and finish by scattering over the mint and pumpkin seeds.

HAWAIIAN MANGO POKE BOATS

SERVES 4

Chicory can be a 'love it or loathe it' type of leaf. While my husband generally struggles with its inherent bitterness, he adores these little poke boats – smoky, sweet and fresh, their intriguing flavour combination often becomes a talking point…for all the right reasons, I might add. The mango's soft flesh absorbs the marinade beautifully while still retaining its all-important form. Having never been to Hawaii myself (it's on the bucket list!), I can't confirm if these resemble the real thing but they do emphatically work – and in the grand scheme of things that's really all that matters.

2 tablespoons tamari
1 tablespoon cold-pressed sesame oil
1 tablespoon maple syrup
juice of ½ orange
1 tablespoon lemon or lime juice
1 large ripe mango, peeled, stone removed
  and cut into bite-sized pieces

2 spring onions, finely chopped
small handful of coriander leaves, roughly
  chopped
1 tablespoon black sesame seeds
1 head of chicory, leaves separated

1. In a bowl, whisk the tamari, sesame oil, maple syrup, orange and lemon juices together vigorously until combined.

2. Add the mango to the bowl and stir to combine, then cover with clingfilm and refrigerate for 1 hour. Remove the mango using a slotted spoon and transfer to a shallow bowl.

3. Add the spring onion, coriander and black sesame seeds to the mango bowl, reserving a little of each for garnish.

4. Arrange the chicory leaves on a large plate or platter. Fill each leaf 'boat' with a spoonful of the mango poke, garnish with the remaining spring onion, coriander and sesame seeds and serve.

SWEETCORN FRITTERS

with quick-pickled carrot

MAKES 8-10 FRITTERS

I'm sure many of you already have a go-to fritter recipe up your sleeve but I still think these are worth your consideration. I try to limit how often I make them because I end up consuming most of them on my own. I also make slightly small versions for parties (they're great finger food) as well as serving them at brunch like this topped with a super-fresh 'quick pickle' and accompanied by tumblers of green juice. I can't think of a better way to kick-start the weekend, can you?

100g canned sweetcorn kernels
75g gram (chickpea) flour
¼ teaspoon baking powder
½ teaspoon sea salt flakes
¼ teaspoon black pepper
juice of 1 lemon
75ml soy milk
1 sweetcorn cob, kernels removed
3 spring onions, chopped
2–3 tablespoons rapeseed oil

Quick-pickled carrot
1 large carrot, cut into fine ribbons
juice of ½ lemon
juice of ½ orange
1 tablespoon cider vinegar
1 tablespoon palm sugar or maple syrup
2 teaspoons sea salt flakes
30g sultanas
1 heaped tablespoon finely chopped fresh
    coriander leaves

1. For the quick-pickled carrot, add the carrot to a shallow bowl together with the lemon and orange juices, cider vinegar, palm sugar and salt. Stir through the sultanas and leave for 1–2 minutes to soak, then mix together with your hands to combine and refrigerate until needed.
2. Add the canned sweetcorn kernels to a blender and blitz to a smooth purée.
3. Whisk the flour, baking powder, salt and pepper together in a large bowl. Add the sweetcorn purée, lemon juice and soy milk and stir together to form a thick batter.
4. Stir the raw sweetcorn kernels and spring onion through the batter and season generously.
5. Heat the rapeseed oil in a large frying pan over a medium–high heat, add tablespoonfuls of the batter to the pan and cook the fritters in batches of two or three for 5 minutes on each side until crispy and golden. Transfer the fritters to a plate lined with kitchen paper to soak up any excess oil.
6. Repeat using all the remaining batter, being sure not to overcrowd the pan as you go.
7. Remove the pickled carrot from the refrigerator and stir through the chopped coriander. Serve alongside the sweetcorn fritters.

MELON, AVOCADO & BUTTER BEAN SALAD

with a jalapeño & lime dressing

SERVES 2-4

This melon and butter bean salad is a recent favourite of mine. Because it works equally well as a side dish as it does as a complete meal, I find myself making it more and more often. The colours are a feast for the eyes and a peculiarly soothing trio – there's something about the soft orange and beige and smattering of pale green that exudes calm.

½ ripe cantaloupe melon, seeds and rind removed and cut lengthways into thick slices
1 large ripe avocado
230g canned butter beans, rinsed and drained
small handful of mint, chopped
1 spring onion, finely sliced

Jalapeño & lime dressing
1 heaped tablespoon minced red jalapeños
1 echalion or banana shallot, finely chopped
juice of 1 small lime
3 tablespoons extra virgin olive oil
½ tablespoon agave nectar, plus extra if necessary
¼ teaspoon sea salt flakes

1. Place the melon and avocado slices on a plate or platter and fan them out to separate them slightly.
2. Place the dressing ingredients in a bowl and whisk vigorously to combine. Season with salt to taste, adding a little more agave nectar for extra sweetness if needed.
3. Put the beans in a shallow dish, pour over half the dressing and toss to combine. Stir through 1 tablespoon of the chopped mint, then spoon the butter beans over the melon and avocado. Drizzle over the remaining dressing and scatter over the spring onion and remaining mint before serving.

POLENTA PIZZA

with spinach & roasted squash

SERVES 4–6

Polenta is a bit of an obsession of my mine. I enjoy it for breakfast, adore it cut into wedges and fried, and think it makes a pretty epic substitute for mash. But this easy pizza crust might just pip everything else to the post when it comes to how best to consume this super-versatile ingredient. Basically a fancy vehicle for toppings, this crispy, crunchy, flavourful base brings a bit of unexpected wow factor to the table. Perfect for parties, it's sure to make even the most low-key affair go off with a bang.

Base
700ml water
175g polenta
1 tablespoon extra virgin olive oil
sea salt flakes and black pepper

Pizza sauce
3 tablespoons passata (sieved tomatoes)
1 heaped tablespoon tomato purée
1 teaspoon oregano
1 garlic clove, minced
½ tablespoon maple syrup
½ tablespoon balsamic vinegar
50ml water
sea salt flakes and black pepper

Toppings
½ butternut squash, peeled and cut into bite-sized pieces
1 heaped teaspoon oregano

1 tablespoon olive oil
200g spinach
2 shallots, sliced
2 heaped tablespoons freshly chopped basil, plus extra to garnish
2 tablespoons pumpkin seeds
2 tablespoons nutritional yeast (optional), plus extra to garnish
sea salt flakes and black pepper

'Cheesy' sunflower seed sauce
70g sunflower seeds
1 small garlic clove, minced
juice of ½ orange
1 teaspoon Dijon mustard
1 teaspoon maple syrup
½ teaspoon sea salt flakes
1 tablespoon nutritional yeast (optional)
125ml water

1. Preheat the oven to 220°C (200°C fan), Gas Mark 7. Line a baking tray with baking paper.
2. For the base, place the measured water in a saucepan and bring to the boil. Generously salt the water, whisk in the polenta and cook over a medium heat, stirring vigorously, for 15–20 minutes, or until it thickens. Add the oil, season and continue to cook, stirring, until it becomes rubbery and pliable.
3. Tip the polenta mixture on to the prepared baking tray and spread it to the edges using a spatula. Transfer to the refrigerator and leave for 30 minutes to firm.
4. Meanwhile, prepare the toppings. Put the squash, oregano and olive oil in a bowl and toss to coat. Season generously and roast for 30 minutes, or until golden and crispy. Remove from the oven and set aside until needed.

5. Increase the heat to 240°C (220°C fan), Gas Mark 9 and bring a large saucepan of water to the boil. Add the spinach to the pan and cook until wilted, then remove with a slotted spoon and squeeze out any excess liquid before mincing to a rough pulp. Season and set aside until needed.

6. To make the pizza sauce, add the passata, tomato purée, oregano, garlic, maple syrup, balsamic vinegar and measured water to a bowl and whisk together to combine. Season and set aside.

7. Once firm, bake the pizza base for 20–25 minutes until the edges begin to crisp.

8. Spread the base with the pizza sauce and top with the sliced shallots, wilted spinach, basil, roasted squash, pumpkin seeds and the nutritional yeast, if using. Bake for a further 15–20 minutes, or until the edges are crispy and golden.

9. Meanwhile, place all the 'cheesy' sauce ingredients in a bowl and whizz together with a hand-held blender until completely smooth.

10. To serve, cut the pizza into squares, drizzle over the sauce and garnish with a little extra basil and/or nutritional yeast.

'MADE IN MINUTES' MINTED PEA MASH

SERVES 2–4

As much as I adore potatoes, sometimes I really do fancy a change. And while peas might not be at the top of most people's lists when asked to name their favourite veg, I think they are something of an underappreciated gem. This purée borders on just the right side of mushy pea, in my opinion, and is the perfect accompaniment to any evening meal, whether it's a pie, roasted celeriac steaks or even marinated tofu. Wonderfully versatile, it can be made and on the table in mere minutes.

1 tablespoon olive oil	250g frozen peas
1 leek, trimmed and sliced	1 heaped tablespoon canned coconut cream
½ vegetable stock cube	1 heaped tablespoon finely chopped mint
1 large garlic clove, unpeeled	sea salt flakes and black pepper
350ml water	

1. Heat the olive oil in a small saucepan over a medium heat. Add the leek, season and sweat for 2–3 minutes until softened.

2. Add the stock cube and garlic clove to the pan, cover with the water and bring to the boil, then add the peas, reduce the heat to a simmer and cook gently for 2–3 minutes until the peas are just cooked through.

3. Drain the peas and transfer to a food processor. Unpeel the garlic clove and add it to the processor together with the coconut cream, then season and pulse until the mixture forms a coarse purée.

4. Return the pea mixture to the pan, stir through the mint and gently heat through before serving.

WARM POTATO & SAMPHIRE SALAD

SERVES 4

When it's in season, I buy samphire by the bucket-load and because it makes a limited appearance I desperately try to make the most of it. Often I'll stir it through freshly cooked pasta before finishing the dish with a squeeze of lemon juice (bliss!), but I'm also partial to it in a warm potato salad. I boil the potatoes first and then let them crisp in the frying pan, which not only saves time but also gives them an almost roast-tatty texture. With the naturally salty samphire, it's a match made in heaven.

500g ruby gem potatoes (or other salad
potatoes)
1 tablespoon rapeseed oil
90g samphire

juice of ½ lemon
2 spring onions, sliced
2 tablespoons finely chopped dill
sea salt flakes and black pepper

1. Add the potatoes to a saucepan of generously salted water, cover with a lid and bring to the boil, then reduce the heat to a gentle simmer and cook for 15–20 minutes, or until tender. Drain and leave to cool for 2–3 minutes before halving.

2. Heat the oil in a large frying pan over a high heat. Add the samphire and stir-fry over a high heat until tender. Season with pepper and squeeze over a little lemon juice, then remove from the pan and set aside.

3. Add the potatoes to the pan cut-side down and fry for 5–10 minutes until crisp, shaking the pan very occasionally but trying not to move them too much as they cook. Season generously.

4. Return the samphire to the pan along with the spring onions. Cook for 2 minutes, then remove from the heat, squeeze over the rest of the lemon juice, stir through the dill and serve.

RAW CURRIED COURGETTE NOODLES

SERVES 2–4

I don't go in for a tremendous amount of spiralizing but when I do it's usually to make this dish. It could be considered something of a 'raw ramen bowl' due to (a) its convenience and (b) its comfort-food credentials – not a duo to be sniffed at. Best eaten fresh, these curried noodles frequently appear on my summer lunchtime menu and, despite the inclusion of mango and dates, the sauce used to coat them manages to remain surprisingly savoury. Even if you have your reservations about raw food, I urge you to give this recipe a go.

2 large courgettes, trimmed
1 ripe mango, peeled, stone removed and sliced
50g soaked cashews
1 yellow pepper, cored and deseeded
2 medjool dates, pitted

2 heaped teaspoons mild curry powder
juice of ½ lime
small bunch of fresh coriander leaves, finely chopped, plus extra to garnish
sea salt flakes and black pepper

1. Using a spiralizer, cut the courgettes into long, thin noodles (or alternatively slice them into thin ribbons using a vegetable peeler). Transfer the noodles to a large bowl.

2. Add the mango, cashews, yellow pepper, dates, curry powder and lime juice to a blender or food processor, season generously and blitz to form a smooth sauce.

3. Pour the sauce over the courgettes and scatter over the coriander. Toss gently until the noodles are completely coated, then divide among bowls and garnish with a little extra chopped coriander. Serve.

SPICE IT UP!

MINI BLACK-BEAN CHIMICHANGAS

with an avocado dip

SERVES 2–3

Black beans and avocado are a timeless pairing, and one I have a particular fondness for. While I've occasionally tampered with the filling and the dip concoction here, nothing comes remotely close to the addictiveness of this combination (garlicky white beans and pesto has been the closest contender). I tend to think the old adage 'if it ain't broke…' is particularly applicable here: not exactly groundbreaking chimichanga territory, but when it tastes this good, who cares?

75ml olive oil
6 taco-sized tortillas

Refried black beans
1 tablespoon olive oil
1 onion, finely chopped
1 garlic clove, minced
300g canned black beans, with their liquid
1 bay leaf
1 tablespoon minced pickled jalapeños
sea salt flakes and black pepper

Avocado dip
½ ripe avocado
1 tablespoon plain coconut or soy yogurt
1 tablespoon tahini
juice of ½ lime
1 garlic clove, minced
sea salt flakes and black pepper

1. For the refried beans, heat the olive oil in a saucepan over a medium heat. Add the onion, season and sweat for 2–3 minutes, or until translucent.

2. Add the garlic to the pan and sauté until aromatic, then add the black beans and their liquid together with the bay leaf and jalapeños. Season generously and simmer for 20 minutes until the mixture is relatively thick and the beans have softened further, then remove from the heat and roughly mash, leaving a few beans whole for texture. Set aside until needed.

3. To make the avocado dip, place the avocado, yogurt, tahini, lime juice and garlic in a blender. Season, add a splash of water and blend until completely smooth. Refrigerate until needed.

4. Heat the olive oil in a small frying pan over a medium–high heat. Add a small piece of tortilla to check the temperature – if it is crispy and golden after 30 seconds then the oil is at the right temperature for frying.

5. Place a tortilla on a work surface, add a spoonful of the black bean mixture to the lower half and tuck in both sides before folding over the nearest edge. Carefully but firmly roll the tortilla up into a log and dampen the edges with a little water to secure. Repeat with the remaining tortillas and filling.

6. Carefully lower the chimichangas into the hot oil in batches and fry for 2–3 minutes on each side until crispy and golden (being careful not to overcrowd the pan). Remove from the pan and drain on a plate lined with kitchen paper, then serve immediately alongside the avocado dip.

SPICE IT UP!

STIR-FRIED SOBA NOODLES

with griddled aubergine medallions

SERVES 2-4

I might have a griddle-pan problem. Whether fruit or veg, it will soon feel the piercingly hot ridges of my well-used turquoise griddle pan. Aubergines lend themselves especially well to a good charring. The miso sauce is rich and satisfying and, well, the soba noodles are a bit of a no-brainer. This is fuss-free food with a touch of panache – and all it requires is a bit of griddle-pan bravery. Go forth and sear!

1 large garlic clove, minced

1 thumb-sized piece of fresh root ginger,
   peeled and minced

1 green chilli, minced

1½ teaspoons Sriracha or other chilli sauce

3 tablespoons tamari or soy sauce

1 tablespoon sesame oil

juice of ½ orange

1 tablespoon lime juice (or lemon juice)

½ tablespoon maple syrup

200g soba noodles

1 tablespoon coconut oil

1 small onion, finely sliced

100g Brussels sprouts, finely sliced

150g cavolo nero, finely sliced

1 heaped tablespoon roughly chopped fresh
   coriander leaves

1 heaped teaspoon dried chilli flakes

sea salt flakes and black pepper

Aubergine medallions

2 tablespoons miso paste

1 tablespoon tamari or soy sauce

1 tablespoon rice mirin

1 tablespoon toasted sesame oil

juice of ½ orange

½ tablespoon maple syrup

1 large aubergine, cut into 1cm rounds

1. For the aubergine medallions, place the miso, tamari, mirin, sesame oil, orange juice and maple syrup in a bowl and whisk vigorously to combine. Add the aubergine rounds and toss to coat evenly, then leave to marinate for 10 minutes.

2. Add the garlic, ginger, chilli, Sriracha, tamari, sesame oil, orange juice, lime juice and maple syrup to a bowl and whisk to combine. Set aside.

3. Put a griddle pan over a medium–high heat. Add the aubergine rounds and griddle for 2–3 minutes on each side until charred, then return to the marinade bowl and brush with any remaining sauce. Cover and keep warm in a low oven.

4. Add the soba noodles to a saucepan of boiling water and cook according to the packet instructions. Drain, rinse and set aside.

5. Melt the coconut oil in a large frying pan over a medium–high heat. Add the onion, sprouts and cavolo nero, season and sauté for 2–3 minutes, or until starting to soften. Add 1½ tablespoons of the sauce and cook, stirring, for a further 2 minutes.

6. Add the soba noodles and the remaining sauce to the pan, toss to combine and heat through, then remove from the heat. Season to taste, adding another splash of tamari if needed, then top with the griddled aubergine, scatter over the coriander and chilli flakes and serve.

BATTERED TOFU FINGERS

with salt & chilli

SERVES 4

If I had a penny for every time someone told me they hated tofu I'd be a very rich woman indeed. What I'd really like to do though is carry a batch of these with me everywhere I go, so I don't have to fruitlessly defend poor tofu's honour and can let the food do the talking instead. The crunchy batter that encases these beauties goes a very long way in showing bean curd off in its best possible light. It also happens to be gluten-free – curiously the coating doesn't work half as well with any other flour. Additional dietary requirements aside, if you're after a tofu recipe to win over dubious friends, may I kindly suggest that you have officially found it.

100g rice flour
1 teaspoon gluten-free baking powder
½ teaspoon garlic powder
1 teaspoon sea salt flakes
1 teaspoon dried chilli flakes
¼ teaspoon black pepper
1 heaped teaspoon brown or palm sugar
125ml water
100ml olive oil
1 x 300g firm tofu block, pressed
    (*see* page 11)

Salt and chilli coating
1 heaped teaspoon fine sea salt
1 teaspoon dried chilli flakes
¼ teaspoon light brown or palm sugar
¼ teaspoon black pepper

1. Put the rice flour, baking powder, garlic powder, sea salt, chilli flakes, black pepper and sugar in a mixing bowl. Stir to combine, then pour in the measured water and whisk to form a batter.
2. Heat the olive oil in a small frying pan over a medium–high heat to 180°C, or until a cube of bread browns in 30 seconds.
3. For the coating, put all the ingredients in a shallow bowl and mix to combine.
4. Cut the tofu block in half and slice the halves lengthways into 2cm (¾in) wide fingers. Dip each finger into the batter, then add them to pan in batches and fry in batches for 2–3 minutes on each side until golden, spooning a little more batter over the pieces before turning and being sure not to overcrowd the pan.
5. Remove the tofu pieces from the pan with tongs and drain on kitchen paper, then lightly dust with the salt and chilli coating. Serve immediately.

FALAFEL SHAKSHUKA

SERVES 4

Falafel is a mainstay in many a vegan's weekly menu plan. A lunchtime fallback and perennial 'we don't know what else to serve you' fave, it's become something of an unofficial running joke in vegan circles. I too was becoming a wee bit tired of consuming yet another falafel-and-salad-stuffed pitta and honestly didn't believe 'poaching' them would make that much difference. Or so I thought. Letting these chickpea-filled beauties steam until fluffy and virtually melt-in-the-mouth delicious in a sauce so good you'll be licking the pan was an absolute revelation. In fact, my love affair with these wondrous little veg-balls has officially been reignited – I'll never look at a falafel the same way again.

1 tablespoon olive oil
1 onion, finely chopped
1 small aubergine, sliced
3 garlic cloves, minced
1 scant teaspoon smoked paprika
¼ teaspoon ground cinnamon
1 tablespoon tomato purée
200g passata (sieved tomatoes)
400g can chopped tomatoes
1 teaspoon dried chilli flakes or 1 red chilli, chopped
pinch of sugar
12 shop-bought falafel
sea salt flakes and black pepper

Tahini sauce
2 tablespoons light tahini
½ tablespoon pomegranate molasses
1 teaspoon agave nectar
juice of ½ lemon
1–2 tablespoons water
pinch of fine sea salt flakes

To serve
8–10 taco-sized tortillas or flatbreads
handful of pomegranate seeds
handful of tarragon, torn

1. Heat the oil in a large frying pan over a medium heat. Add the onion to the pan, season and sweat for 2–3 minutes until it begins to soften.

2. Add the aubergine and stir to combine. Sauté for 2–3 minutes, then add the garlic, sprinkle over the smoked paprika and cinnamon and stir to coat. Cover and cook for another 2–3 minutes, or until the aubergine has started to soften.

3. Add the tomato purée, passata and chopped tomatoes to the pan. Fill the tomato can with water and add it to the sauce together with the chilli and sugar. Season generously and simmer uncovered for about 20 minutes, or until the sauce is rich and bubbling.

4. Place the falafel in the pan, making sure not to cover them with the sauce – they should be peeking out! Cover and simmer gently for a further 10 minutes.

5. Meanwhile, make the tahini sauce by whisking the ingredients together in a small bowl until smooth and glossy.

6. Griddle or toast the tortillas and keep warm under a clean tea towel.

7. To serve, drizzle the tahini sauce over the shakshuka and garnish with the pomegranate seeds and tarragon. Put the pan in the centre of the table along with the tortillas and let everyone help themselves.

MY FAVOURITE PENNE ALLA NORMA

SERVES 4

There are few things that give me more pleasure in life than a bowl of freshly cooked pasta, especially when paired with some sort of tomato sauce. In this case, I've opted for fresh tomatoes rather than canned, and I really think it makes a difference. Once simmered and reduced, this sauce is the perfect accompaniment to a simple dish of Sicilian origin – although I have to admit I have (a) never set foot in Sicily and (b) have zero claim to this being in any way authentic. I should be mortified but I'm not. In fact, I'm sure most Sicilians would recoil in horror at the very thought of 'tofu ricotta', but once you get over that mental hurdle, you'll be able to fully appreciate what is really a rather lovely dish. Enjoy!

1 tablespoon olive oil
1 onion, sliced
1 aubergine, roughly chopped
3 garlic cloves, minced
1 heaped teaspoon oregano
1 heaped tablespoon tomato purée
400g tomatoes, diced
1 large red chilli, minced
1 tablespoon balsamic vinegar
250ml water
300g penne
1 tablespoon capers, minced
sea salt flakes and black pepper

Tofu ricotta
250g firm tofu
1 large garlic clove, grated
grated zest and juice of ½ lemon
3 tablespoons extra virgin olive oil
1 teaspoon sea salt flakes
black pepper

To serve
basil leaves, torn
extra virgin olive oil

1. To make the tofu ricotta, place all the ingredients in a food processor and pulse until everything is combined and the mixture has a smooth, ricotta-like texture (be careful not to blend it too finely). Season to taste and refrigerate until needed.

2. Heat the olive oil in a large frying pan over a medium heat. Add the onion, season and sweat for 4–5 minutes until softened and translucent.

3. Add the aubergine to the pan and sauté for 2–3 minutes until it begins to soften. Add the garlic, oregano, tomato purée and a splash of water and cook, stirring, for a further 1–2 minutes, then add the tomatoes, chilli, balsamic vinegar and measured water and simmer for 30 minutes, stirring occasionally, until the sauce has thickened and reduced.

4. Meanwhile, bring a large saucepan of salted water to the boil, add the penne and cook for a few minutes under the recommended cooking time on the packet. Drain and stir into the sauce with the capers, season with salt and pepper and cook, stirring, for 5 minutes.

5. Remove from the heat and divide among bowls, spooning over the tofu ricotta, scattering over a few torn basil leaves and drizzling generously with extra virgin olive oil to finish. Serve.

CURRIED CORIANDER PARSNIP SOUP

with roasted cashews

SERVES 2-4

It always baffles (borderline offends) me when people tell me they think soup is boring. Perhaps it's my ultra-Irish upbringing but nothing manages to conjure up a better image of warmth and comfort to me than a steaming bowl of soup. This simple parsnip soup is spiked with just the right amount of spice to re-enforce those well-entrenched memories…although granted, my childhood was less about curried anything and more about cream of tomato. Regardless, the sentiment remains the same and even though this recipe strays a little from tradition (roasted cashews will do that do a dish) this humble bowl has a reassuringly similar effect.

½ tablespoon coconut oil

1 small leek, trimmed, cleaned and roughly chopped

6 parsnips, peeled and chopped

2 garlic cloves, minced

1 thumb-sized piece of fresh root ginger, peeled and minced

1 teaspoon garam masala

1 teaspoon ground cumin

½ teaspoon mild curry powder

¼ teaspoon ground turmeric

¼ teaspoon cayenne powder (or chilli powder)

½ tablespoon maple syrup

1 vegetable stock cube

1 kaffir lime leaf

750ml water

large bunch of fresh coriander, chopped

sea salt flakes and black pepper

To serve

roasted cashews

chopped fresh coriander leaves

soy cream (optional)

1. Melt the coconut oil in a heavy-based saucepan over a medium heat. Add the leek to the pan and sauté gently until slightly softened but not coloured, then add the parsnips, garlic and ginger. Cook, stirring, over a low heat for 2–3 minutes, or until nicely aromatic.

2. Add the spices and maple syrup, stir to coat and fry for a further 2–3 minutes, then add the stock cube, lime leaf and 500ml of the water. Bring to a gentle simmer and cook for around 20 minutes, or until the parsnip is soft.

3. Remove and discard the lime leaf, transfer the soup to a blender or food processor with the chopped coriander and blend until completely smooth, then return the soup to the pan, add the remaining 250ml water and heat gently. Season to taste.

4. Serve in warmed bowls garnished with roasted cashews, chopped coriander and swirls of soy cream, if you like.

BLACK-EYED PEA STEW

with buckwheat pancakes & fried plantain

SERVES 2

I have a difficult relationship with buckwheat. I desperately want to love it but am often left feeling slightly underwhelmed. For this book I was determined to find a way to best utilize this naturally gluten-free grain (which is, somewhat confusingly, actually a seed) and these crêpe-like pancakes are the pleasing result. You can buy ready-ground buckwheat flour but I find grinding my own makes for a better crêpe – I also like to use buckwheat flakes in porridge, so tend to have them lying around. Getting these pancakes as thin as possible might take some practice. I find a rubber spatula helpful, letting me ease the batter to the edges of the pan. These pancakes also make terrific wraps, so if you have any left over, fill them with hummus and fresh veggies for lunch.

2 tablespoons olive oil
1 onion, sliced
1 celery stick, sliced
1 red pepper, cored, deseeded and sliced
3 garlic cloves, minced
1 tablespoon red jalapeños, minced
1 heaped teaspoon chipotle paste
200ml canned coconut milk
300g canned black-eyed beans, drained
  and rinsed
sea salt flakes and black pepper

Buckwheat pancakes
100g buckwheat flakes or flour

several thyme sprigs, leaves stripped
¼ teaspoon bicarbonate of soda
juice of ½ lemon
150–175ml water
sea salt flakes and black pepper

Fried plantain
50ml rapeseed oil
1 large ripe plantain, sliced diagonally
¼ teaspoon sea salt flakes

To serve
1 ripe avocado, sliced
basil leaves, torn

1. For the pancakes, place the buckwheat, thyme leaves and bicarbonate of soda in a blender or food processor. Season and blitz until the mixture forms a fine flour, then transfer to a large mixing bowl, add the lemon juice and water and whisk together to form a batter with the consistency of single cream. Set aside until needed.

2. Heat 1 tablespoon of the olive oil in a frying pan over a medium heat. Add the onion, celery and red pepper, season and fry until the vegetables begin to soften.

3. Add the garlic and jalapeños, stir to combine and gently fry until aromatic, then stir in the chipotle paste and coconut milk. Season and bring to a gentle simmer. Cook for 10 minutes, then add the beans and simmer for a further 5 minutes, or until the sauce has thickened and reduced. Cover with a lid and set aside.

4. Set a crêpe pan over a medium heat and brush it with 1 teaspoon of olive oil. Ladle a third of the batter into the pan and immediately spread it to the edges using a spatula, then cook for 3–4 minutes,

or until the edges come away easily. Flip the pancake over and cook for a further 30 seconds, then transfer to a dish and cover with a clean tea towel. Repeat until all the batter is used, adding another teaspoon or so of oil to the pan between each pancake.

5. To make the fried plantain, heat the rapeseed oil in a frying pan over a medium–high heat, add the plantain slices and fry for 2–3 minutes on each side until golden. Transfer to a plate lined with kitchen paper and sprinkle with sea salt.

6. To serve, fold the pancakes over crêpe suzette-style and top with the stew, fried plantain, sliced avocado and torn basil leaves. Alternatively, fill and roll them up like fajitas, placing the individual dishes in the centre of the table and letting everyone help themselves.

SWEET POTATO HASH BROWNS

with a chipotle soured cream

SERVES 2-4

These sweet potato hash browns are seriously addictive. Piled high into the pan they soon reduce to a crispy mass of yumminess – a stripped back fritter, if you will. It helps to have a very wide spatula for flipping and make sure your pan is suitably nonstick to avoid any would-be disasters. Served alongside this smoky chipotle cashew cream they are a mega weekend treat that will be sure to become a firm brunch favourite.

2 large sweet potatoes, grated or spiralized
2 teaspoons ground cumin
1 teaspoon ground coriander
½ teaspoon ground cinnamon
1–1½ tablespoons coconut oil
sea salt flakes and black pepper
1 tablespoon chopped chives, to garnish

Chipotle soured cream
100g cashew nuts, soaked and drained (*see* page 8)
1 tablespoon cider vinegar
juice of ½ lemon
pinch of sea salt flakes
75–100ml water
1 tablespoon chipotle paste

1. For the chipotle soured cream, place the cashew nuts in a blender along with the cider vinegar, lemon juice, salt and 75ml of water. Blend until it is completely smooth, scraping down the sides periodically and adding a little more water if necessary. Once smooth, add the chipotle paste and blend to combine. Check for seasoning and refrigerate until needed.

2. Add the sweet potato and spices to a large mixing bowl, season with salt and pepper and toss to combine.

3. Melt 1 heaped teaspoon of coconut oil in a frying pan over a medium heat. Add a large handful of the grated sweet potato mixture and press it down firmly using a spatula to form a rough circle. Repeat with a few more handfuls (you want to be careful not to overcrowd the pan, so it's best to cook these in batches). Fry for 5 minutes on each side, pressing down firmly on the hash browns with the spatula to help them bind together, until the edges begin to crisp.

4. Repeat until all the sweet potato has been used, adding a touch more coconut oil to the pan each time (the mixture should give around eight large hash browns). Divide among plates and serve immediately with a decent dollop of the chipotle soured cream and some chopped chives to garnish.

BUTTER BEAN JALFREZI

SERVES 4

We all need a go-to weeknight meal and for me this is it. On the table in 30 minutes, it's rammed full of flavour and rates pretty well on the health-o-meter too. In many cases beans are interchangeable but I think these large circular butter bean discs add a meaty texture here that really can't be replicated with any other legume. I typically serve this with freshly boiled basmati but it would also be wonderful with any type of flatbread – both would be even better.

½ tablespoon coconut oil

1 celery stick, minced

3 garlic cloves, minced

1 thumb-sized piece of fresh root ginger, peeled and minced

2 green chillies, minced

1 red pepper, cored, deseeded and roughly chopped

1 yellow pepper, cored, deseeded and roughly chopped

1 green pepper, cored, deseeded and roughly chopped

1 heaped teaspoon garam masala

1 teaspoon ground cumin

½ teaspoon ground coriander

½ teaspoon ground turmeric

1 x 400g can plum tomatoes

1 tablespoon tomato purée

1 teaspoon brown sugar

1 kaffir lime leaf (or bay leaf)

400g can butter beans, rinsed and drained

juice of ½ lime

3 tablespoons soy or coconut cream (optional)

sea salt flakes and black pepper

small bunch of fresh coriander, roughly chopped, to garnish

basmati rice, to serve

1. Heat the coconut oil in a large saucepan over a medium heat. Add the celery, garlic, ginger and chilli and fry gently until nicely aromatic.

2. Add the peppers to the pan, sprinkle over the spices and season generously. Stir to coat then cook, stirring, for 2–3 minutes until the peppers begin to soften.

3. Add the tomatoes to the pan and break them up using the back of a spoon. Stir through the tomato purée and season generously, then add the sugar and lime leaf and bring to a gentle simmer. Cover and cook for 20 minutes, until the peppers are cooked through.

4. Stir in the butter beans and cook uncovered for a further 10 minutes, or until the sauce has thickened and reduced. Add the lime juice and soy cream, if using, and simmer for a further 1–2 minutes. Remove from the heat.

5. To serve, divide among bowls and scatter over the coriander to garnish. Accompany with freshly boiled basmati rice.

EASY KOREAN RAMEN BOWL

SERVES 4

The success of this dish hinges entirely on the sauce. Who knew that peanut butter and gochujang (a fiery hot Korean paste) would be such a formidable pairing? I was so taken with it when I first discovered it that I made this dish (or a variation on it) every week for almost six months. Nothing could take the sheen off this number; I couldn't get enough. Should you wish to forgo the ramen element, feel free, because truthfully this recipe is also magnificent with steamed white rice – just don't put it underneath the sauce or else it will be swamped.

½ tablespoon coconut oil

1 red onion, roughly chopped

1 large carrot, sliced diagonally

1 large parsnip, sliced diagonally

2 tablespoons gochujang (Korean chilli paste)

1 tablespoon miso paste

1 tablespoon smooth peanut butter

½ tablespoon soy sauce, plus extra if needed

½ tablespoon maple syrup

1.5 litres water

15 x 10cm piece of kombu seaweed

handful of green beans, halved

½ head of cauliflower, broken into florets

100g firm tofu, cut into cubes

250g fine rice noodle nests

sea salt flakes

Quick pickled cucumber

1 small cucumber, halved lengthways and
    sliced into ribbons

½ tablespoon sugar

½ tablespoon sea salt flakes

juice of ½ lime (or lemon)

½ tablespoon Zingy Yuzu and Miso Dressing
    (see page 18)

1 teaspoon dried chilli flakes

1 tablespoon black sesame seeds

To serve

2 spring onions, sliced

small handful of fresh coriander leaves,
    roughly chopped

1 nori seaweed sheet, shredded

1. To make the pickled cucumber, add the cucumber pieces to a shallow bowl, sprinkle over the sugar and salt and pour over the lime juice and yuzu dressing. Toss to combine and set aside until needed.

2. Heat the coconut oil in a large heavy-based saucepan over a medium heat. Add the onion, carrot and parsnip to the pan, season with a little salt and sauté for 1–2 minutes until slightly softened.

3. Add the gochujang, miso, smooth peanut butter, soy sauce and maple syrup to the pan, pour over the measured water and stir in the kombu.

4. Bring to the boil, then reduce the heat to a simmer and cook for 5–7 minutes. Remove the kombu and finely slice, then add to the pan with the beans and cauliflower and cook for a further 10 minutes. Add the tofu and cook for 5 minutes to warm through. Season with salt, adding a splash of soy sauce if needed.

5. Divide the rice noodle nests among 4 deep bowls, then ladle over the stew so that the noodles are fully submerged. Leave the noodles for 2–3 minutes to soften in the broth before using chopsticks to break them up further and mix everything together thoroughly.

6. Stir the chilli flakes and sesame seeds through the quick pickled cucumber and use it to top the ramen bowls together with the spring onion, coriander and nori. Serve.

SPICE IT UP!

'CHIP-SHOP' VEGETABLE CURRY

SERVES 4

If you grew up in the UK or Ireland, you'll no doubt be familiar with that late-night takeaway special, the incomparable 'half and half'. For those unfamiliar with the concept, it's a terribly inauthentic curry served with 'half chips, half rice'. Sounds vile, but after a heavy night on the tiles it's almost akin to salvation. You could say then that this is my homage to not only the curry that saved me from many a chronic hangover but also to those heady days that were wonderful at the time but which I have absolutely no desire to revisit.

1 tablespoon coconut oil

1 onion, roughly chopped

2 garlic cloves, minced

1 thumb-sized piece of fresh root ginger, peeled and minced

1 green chilli, minced

200g mushrooms, trimmed and sliced

½ head of cauliflower, broken into small florets

1 heaped teaspoon garam masala

1 teaspoon ground cumin

½ teaspoon ground coriander

½ teaspoon ground turmeric

½ tablespoon palm or brown sugar

1 heaped tablespoon cornflour

500ml water

1 heaped tablespoon tomato purée

2 kaffir lime leaves

200ml canned coconut milk

75g frozen peas

100g spinach, blanched and chopped

sea salt flakes and black pepper

1. Heat the coconut oil in a large pan over a medium heat. Add the onion, season with salt and pepper and sweat for 3–4 minutes, until translucent.

2. Add the garlic, ginger and chilli to the pan and sauté for 2–3 minutes, or until aromatic.

3. Add the mushrooms to the pan, season generously and cook over a medium–high heat for 5 minutes, or until the mushrooms begin to colour, release their juices and shrink.

4. Add the cauliflower florets to the pan together with the spices, sugar and a splash of water. Cook for 1–2 minutes before sprinkling over the cornflour and stirring to coat evenly.

5. Pour over the measured water and stir continuously until the sauce thickens, then add the tomato purée and lime leaves.

6. Bring to a simmer, cover and leave to cook for 20 minutes, then stir in the coconut milk, peas and spinach. Season generously and simmer for a further 10–15 minutes, uncovered, until thickened and reduced. Season to taste and serve.

SWEET 'N' STICKY CAULIFLOWER FLORETS

with a cooling coconut dip

SERVES 4

Whether it's griddled, baked, or even blitzed into 'rice', I've found a multitude of uses for cauliflower but none of them have quite had that 'knock-yer-socks-off' effect that this one possesses. Gochujang may seem like a speciality ingredient but thankfully it's now widely available in supermarkets. I guarantee this spicy Korean paste will soon become a staple – I like to dollop it into stews to boost flavour. Think of this as the ultimate cauliflower dish that'll have you coming back for more.

70g panko breadcrumbs
1 head of cauliflower, broken into florets

Batter
70g gram (chickpea) or rice flour
pinch of sea salt flakes
¼ teaspoon garlic powder
¼ teaspoon white pepper
¼ teaspoon bicarbonate of soda
juice of ½ lemon
150ml soy milk

Gochujang dressing
2 heaped tablespoons gochujang (Korean red chilli paste)

2 tablespoons soy sauce
1 tablespoon cider (or rice wine) vinegar
3 tablespoons maple syrup
50ml water, plus extra if necessary

Cooling coconut dipping sauce
150g coconut yogurt
1 garlic clove, minced
grated zest and juice of 1 lemon
1 teaspoon cider vinegar
pinch of pink Himalayan salt or sea salt flakes

To serve
½ cucumber, finely sliced
1 tablespoon black sesame seeds

1. Preheat the oven to 240°C (220°C fan), Gas Mark 9 and line a baking tray with foil or baking paper.
2. Place the ingredients for the coconut dipping sauce in a blender and blitz together until smooth (alternatively, vigorously whisk them together in a bowl until combined). Refrigerate until needed.
3. To make the batter, whisk the ingredients together in a bowl until smooth.
4. Place the panko breadcrumbs in a food processor and pulse briefly to break up any large pieces. Transfer to a separate bowl.
5. Dip a cauliflower floret first in the batter and shake off any excess before dredging in the panko crumbs and placing on the prepared baking tray. Repeat with the rest of the florets, then bake for 25 minutes, turning once, until crispy and golden.
6. Meanwhile, place the gochujang dressing ingredients in a saucepan, bring to the boil and cook for 2–3 minutes, or until smooth and glossy, adding a splash more water if the dressing looks as though it is getting too thick. Keep warm over a low heat.
7. Transfer the baked cauliflower to a large bowl, pour over the dressing and toss to coat, then scatter over the cucumber slices and sesame seeds to finish. Serve with the coconut dipping sauce.

SPICE IT UP!

HARISSA-COATED TOFU KEBABS

SERVES 4

If you're of the common opinion that tofu is bland then this is absolutely the recipe to change your mind. It's funny how a handful of familiar ingredients can transform a slab of bean curd into something even your average meat-eater would devour (no mean feat, I can tell you), although be prepared for the predictable round of tofu jokes. I'm fairly certain I've heard them all by this stage. Harissa paste is a trusty staple in my pantry and is made for marinades, in my opinion. Here it is an absolute godsend, raising the tofu bar to next-level greatness and rendering most naysayers speechless in the process. I love the 'lollipop' kitschness of the skewers, which helps make them a must-have at any summer barbecue, served alongside a bounty of sides and salads. Vegan or not, these are sure to be a fiery hit.

1 x 400g firm tofu block, pressed
  (*see* page 11)
2 tablespoons harissa paste
juice of ½ lemon

1 tablespoon olive oil
½ tablespoon agave nectar
pinch of sea salt flakes

1. Cut the tofu block in half and slice the halves lengthways into 2cm wide fingers.
2. Combine the harissa, lemon juice, oil, agave nectar and salt in a shallow bowl and whisk vigorously to combine. Add the tofu to the bowl and turn to coat, then transfer to the refrigerator and leave to marinate for 1–2 hours.
3. Heat a griddle pan or barbecue to medium–high. Gently push a bamboo skewer through each of the tofu fingers, transfer to the awaiting pan or barbecue and cook for 5–7 minutes on each side until nicely charred.
4. Brush over any remaining marinade and serve with a salad.

TABASCO-DRENCHED TOMATOES

SERVES 4

I have such fondness for roasted tomatoes. They can be served with a multitude of dishes but I prefer them simply on freshly toasted bread – slices of nutty rye are especially good. I like to cut them into wedges, not only because they are easier to eat but also because there's more surface area to carry the array of in-your-face flavours. I've called for one teaspoon of Tabasco sauce in this recipe, but if I'm being totally honest I usually add a touch more. If you think you're brave enough (and after all, they really should be 'drenched' in Tabasco) then I heartily recommend two.

3 large tomatoes

6 garlic cloves

1 tablespoon tamari

1 tablespoon balsamic vinegar

1 tablespoon olive oil

½ tablespoon date syrup

1 teaspoon Tabasco sauce

pinch of dried chilli flakes

sea salt flakes and black pepper

rye bread, to serve

1. Preheat the oven to 220°C (200°C fan), Gas Mark 7.

2. Cut the tomatoes into wedges and place them in an ovenproof dish along with the garlic cloves in their skins.

3. Drizzle the tamari, balsamic vinegar, olive oil, date syrup and Tabasco over the tomatoes, season with salt and pepper and sprinkle over the chilli flakes. Roast for 30 minutes until wrinkled and lightly browned.

4. Serve the tomatoes on top of thick slices of toasted rye bread spread with the roasted garlic, squeezed from its skins.

SPICY MUSHROOM-STUFFED CALZONE

MAKES 4

What's better than a pizza? A pizza that has been stuffed, folded and crimped, of course! And filled with spicy, creamy mushrooms? Even better. There are several elements to this recipe, putting it in the 'at your leisure' category – that is, one of those dishes best reserved for a quiet weekend rather than a manic Tuesday evening. Of course, you could also make the dough ahead of time, and thankfully these calzones also reheat well too. If I want to serve them at gatherings, I bake them until cooked but not crispy and then finish them off in a hot oven when my guests arrive.

1 teaspoon fast-action dried yeast
140ml warm water
1 tablespoon olive oil
1 tablespoon agave nectar or maple syrup
200g plain flour
1 heaped teaspoon sea salt flakes

Mushrooms
1 tablespoon olive oil
300g chestnut mushrooms, trimmed and roughly chopped
1 green chilli, chopped
1 garlic clove, minced
3 spring onions, sliced
1 x Cashew Soured Cream (*see* page 10)
sea salt flakes and black pepper

1. Add the yeast and warm water to a jug, stir and set aside for 10 minutes until foaming, then add the oil and agave nectar and whisk lightly to combine.

2. Place the flour and salt in a large mixing bowl or stand mixer, gradually add the yeast mixture and mix together to form a rough dough. Turn the dough out on to a floured surface and knead for 10 minutes until smooth and elastic, then return it to the bowl with a little oil, cover with a clean tea towel and leave in a warm place to rise for up to 2 hours, or until doubled in size.

3. For the mushrooms, heat the olive oil in a large frying pan over a medium–high heat. Add the mushrooms to the pan, season and sauté until they release their juices and begin to soften, about 5–7 minutes. Add the chilli and garlic and cook for another 5 minutes, then stir through the spring onions, season generously and cook over a low heat for a further 1–2 minutes. Pour over the cashew cream and gently heat through. Once the sauce has thickened slightly, take the pan off the heat and set aside to cool.

4. Preheat the oven to its highest setting – usually around 250°C – and place an upturned baking sheet on to the top shelf (this will act as your pizza stone).

5. Tip the dough on to a floured surface and knead lightly a few times before dividing into four even-sized pieces. Shape each piece into a ball before rolling out into rough oval shapes. Divide the mushroom and cashew cream mixture among the ovals, placing it on one side of the dough only, then fold the dough over and crimp the edges using wetted fingertips to seal in the filling. Lightly dust each calzone with a little flour.

6. Lightly dust the preheated baking tray with flour, then transfer the calzone to the tray and bake for 20–25 minutes, or until the calzone begin to brown and crisp. Serve immediately.

SPICE IT UP!

GRAINS & GOODNESS

QUINOA-STUFFED TOMATOES

SERVES 4–6

Tomatoes might be my favourite fruit. Endlessly versatile, they are an absolute mainstay in my kitchen and, whether canned or fresh, they form the basis of so many of my meals. Here though they really get to shine, becoming the vehicles for a simple but tasty quinoa filling. These stuffed tomatoes can be wheeled out for an easy lunch or served as part of a potluck dinner or buffet – tasting equally wonderful cold as fresh out of the oven makes them a great option for stress-free hosting. For a rather adorable (and delicious) starter, serve them nestled on top of some dressed leaves.

100g quinoa (any colour)
200ml water
2 tablespoons olive oil
1 red onion, finely chopped
1 courgette, diced
grated zest and juice of ½ lemon
100g fresh or frozen sweetcorn kernels
50g frozen peas, defrosted
1 heaped tablespoon vegan pesto, homemade
  (*see* page 141) or shop-bought

30g chopped cashews
6 large tomatoes
sea salt flakes and black pepper

To serve

small handful of mint, chopped
small handful of flat leaf parsley, chopped

1. Add the quinoa to a saucepan and pour over the measured water. Cover with a lid and bring to the boil, then reduce the heat to a simmer and cook for 8–10 minutes, or until all the liquid has been absorbed. Remove from the heat and leave to steam, covered, for 5 minutes, then fluff the quinoa grains up with a fork and set aside (this can be prepared up to a day in advance and kept in a suitable container in the refrigerator until needed).

2. Preheat the oven to 220°C (200°C fan), Gas Mark 7.

3. Heat 1 tablespoon of the olive oil in a frying pan over a medium heat. Add the onion, season generously and sweat for 4–5 minutes until translucent. Add the courgette and lemon zest and cook, stirring, for 5–7 minutes until the courgette begins to soften.

4. Stir through the quinoa, sweetcorn, peas and lemon juice and season. Cook for 2–3 minutes to heat through before stirring through the pesto and cashews. Remove from the heat.

5. Use a sharp knife to cut the tops from the tomatoes (being sure to reserve them) and hollow out the seeds and membranes using a spoon.

6. Spoon the quinoa mixture into the tomatoes, pressing down gently on the filling as you go. Transfer to a baking dish, pop the tops back on, drizzle with the remaining olive oil and season.

7. Bake for 20 minutes until lightly charred and blistered, then remove from the oven and set aside for 5 minutes to cool slightly. Divide among plates and garnish with a little chopped mint and parsley.

SUMMERY SPELT SALAD

with roasted cauliflower & grapes

SERVES 4

I don't use spelt enough. However, each time I make this dish I'm reminded how much I adore this wonderful grain. If you have never roasted grapes before, you'll be surprised at how magnificent they are all blistered and bruised and bursting with flavour. I really should do it more often.

200g spelt grains, soaked overnight and rinsed
½ large cucumber, cut into ribbons
2 tablespoons cider vinegar
1 tablespoon agave nectar
½ teaspoon sea salt flakes
small bunch of dill, finely chopped, plus extra torn fronds to serve
handful of pomegranate seeds, to garnish

Roasted cauliflower & grapes
1 small head of cauliflower, broken into florets
1 tablespoon olive oil

1 heaped teaspoon za'atar (or dried thyme)
50g seedless black grapes

Dressing
75g sunflower
150–175ml water
1 teaspoon Dijon mustard
juice of ½ lemon
½ tablespoon pomegranate molasses
½ tablespoon agave nectar or maple syrup
sea salt flakes and black pepper

1. Add the spelt grains to a large saucepan and pour over 750ml water. Cover and bring to the boil, then reduce the heat to a simmer and cook for 1–1¼ hours, or until all the liquid has been absorbed. Remove from the heat and leave to steam, covered, for 5–10 minutes, then fluff the grains up with a fork and set aside to cool completely.

2. Preheat the oven to 220°C (200°C fan), Gas Mark 7.

3. Put the cauliflower florets in a bowl with the olive oil, toss to coat and sprinkle over the za'atar. Season generously, arrange on a baking tray in an even layer and roast for 15 minutes, then add the grapes and roast for a further 5 minutes, or until the cauliflower is lightly charred and the grapes are blistered.

4. Meanwhile, put the cucumber ribbons in a bowl. Whisk the cider vinegar, agave nectar and salt together in a separate bowl, then pour over the cucumber ribbons and set aside for 15–20 minutes to lightly pickle.

5. Place the cooled spelt in a shallow serving bowl together with a tablespoon or so of the cucumber pickling liquid. Drain the cucumber, add it to the bowl with the dill and toss everything together with your hands to combine.

6. To make the dressing, place all the ingredients in a blender and blitz until completely smooth, scraping down the sides from time to time as you go.

7. To serve, top the salad with the roasted cauliflower and grapes, drizzle over the dressing and garnish with the pomegranate seeds and a few torn dill fronds to finish.

MEGA MISO FREEKEH BOWL

SERVES 2

Miso is a miracle worker when it comes to injecting serious flavour. If ever I'm in search of that extra something, I know that a little knob of this salty paste will come to the rescue and knock it right out of the park. If you can't get your hands on smoked freekeh (or even freekeh for that matter) don't panic – the arguably more accessible bulgur wheat will do an equally fine job. There's always a solution to any food-related problem. Just don't omit the miso.

½ tablespoon coconut oil
½ red onion, finely chopped
150g smoked freekeh (or bulgur wheat)
2 tablespoons miso paste
500ml water
1 large carrot, grated
1 large parsnip, grated
100g kale, leaves torn and stems removed
juice of ½ lemon

2 large medjool dates, pitted and chopped
1 tablespoon toasted peanuts
sea salt flakes and black pepper

To serve
200g steamed purple sprouting broccoli
1 x Goes-with-Everything' Tahini Sauce
  (see page 151)

1. Melt the oil in a large frying pan over a medium heat. Add the onion, season and sauté for 4–5 minutes until softened and slightly coloured.
2. Add the freekeh and miso paste to the pan, pour over the measured water and stir gently until the paste has dissolved. Bring to a simmer and cook, uncovered and stirring occasionally, for 20–25 minutes, or until most of the liquid has been absorbed and the grains are tender but still retaining some bite.
3. Add the carrot and parsnip to the pan, stir to combine and cover with a lid. Reduce the heat to low and cook gently for 1–2 minutes, then stir in the kale and lemon juice and cook, covered, for a further 2–3 until the kale is wilted.
4. Remove from the heat and stir through the dates and peanuts, then divide between bowls. Serve with steamed broccoli and my 'goes-with-everything' tahini sauce.

CAJUN KIDNEY BEAN & BROWN RICE BROTH

SERVES 4

I had previously entitled this simple bowl of goodness 'Soothing Kidney Bean & Brown Rice Broth' because it has a curiously Zen-like ability to rectify even the most stressful of days. I love the smoky heat from the paprika and cayenne combo, which provides just enough kick without being too overpowering. This is bowl food for the soul with the added bonus of being an absolute cinch to make. I like to make a batch at the start of the week and dip into it for lunch or dinner, or alternatively freeze it and reheat servings as and when needed. It also makes a terrific, warming appetizer for any laid-back gathering – simply ladle into mugs and serve.

1 tablespoon olive oil

1 red onion, finely chopped

3 garlic cloves, minced

1 red chilli, minced

¼ teaspoon cayenne pepper

¼ teaspoon garlic powder

1 teaspoon ground cumin

1 teaspoon smoked paprika

200g passata (sieved tomatoes)

1 litre vegetable stock

200g brown rice

400g can kidney beans, rinsed and drained

100g kale, leaves torn and stems removed

½ tablespoon balsamic vinegar

sea salt flakes and black pepper

To serve

1 ripe avocado, sliced

handful of salad cress

a few splashes of Tabasco sauce

1. Heat the olive oil in a heavy-based saucepan over a low heat. Add the onion to the pan, season and sauté for 5 minutes until beginning to soften, then add the garlic and chilli and sauté for a further 3–4 minutes, or until the onion becomes translucent.

2. Mix the spices together in a small bowl, add them to the pan and stir to coat. Pour over the passata and vegetable stock and bring to a boil, then add the brown rice and reduce to a gentle simmer. Cook for 30 minutes, or until the rice is cooked through.

3. Add the kidney beans, kale and balsamic vinegar to the pan and cook for a further 10 minutes, or until the kale wilts. Season to taste.

4. Divide the broth among bowls and top each with a few avocado slices, some salad cress and a splash of Tabasco before serving.

WARMING RED PEPPER SOUP

with crispy polenta wedges

SERVES 4

Perhaps it's because I'm a sucker for all things soup that this is up there with some of my favourite dishes, though there's something about this piercingly hot red pepper number coupled with the perfectly seasoned crisp polenta wedges that makes it a dish to remember. Even though this dish has an air of winter about it, my best memory attached to it (yes, I have an embarrassingly catalogue-like recollection for 'when', 'where' and 'with whom' I ate certain foods) involves sitting outside on a searing hot summer's day with new friends and lots of laughter. Such a simple dish and a simple moment, but so lovely too.

1 tablespoon olive oil

2 small onions, chopped

4 garlic cloves, minced

5 large red peppers, cored, deseeded and
    roughly chopped

1 heaped tablespoon tomato purée

200g passata (sieved tomatoes)

¼ teaspoon Tabasco sauce

1 tablespoon maple syrup

500ml water

sea salt flakes and black pepper

1 tablespoon roughly chopped curly parsley,
    to garnish

Crispy polenta wedges

750ml water

1 vegetable stock cube

100g polenta

juice of ½ lemon

2 tablespoons olive oil

1 teaspoon dried chilli flakes

sea salt flakes and black pepper

1.   Line a 30 x 20cm brownie tin with baking paper.

2.   For the polenta wedges, bring the measured water to the boil in a large saucepan. Add the stock cube and stir to dissolve, then gradually whisk in the polenta and reduce the heat to a low simmer. Cook, stirring continuously, for 15–20 minutes, or until the polenta becomes thick and rubbery, then stir in the lemon juice and 1 tablespoon of the olive oil. Remove from the heat and spoon into the prepared tin, spreading it out evenly to the edges with a spatula. Cover with clingfilm and refrigerate for 2–3 hours, or until firm.

3.   Heat the olive oil in a heavy-based saucepan over a low heat. Add the onions, season and sweat for 2–3 minutes until they begin to soften, then stir in the garlic and sauté for a further 5–7 minutes, or until the onion is translucent.

4.   Add the chopped peppers to the pan, season generously with salt and pepper and sauté for 2–3 minutes, then add the tomato purée, passata, Tabasco, maple syrup and measured water. Season again and bring to a gentle simmer, then cover with a lid and cook for 20–25 minutes, or until the peppers are soft.

5.   Transfer the mixture to a blender or food processor and blend until completely smooth, then return the mixture to the pan. Keep warm.

6. Remove the polenta from the refrigerator and slice it into eighths before halving each slice diagonally into triangles.

7. Heat a griddle pan over a medium–high heat and lightly brush it with the remaining oil. Add the polenta wedges and griddle for 3–4 minutes on each side until crispy, golden and lightly marked. Transfer to a dish, sprinkle over the chilli flakes and season to taste.

8. Check the soup for seasoning before dividing among warmed bowls, adding a couple of polenta wedges and a scattering of parsley to each before serving.

AUBERGINE INVOLTINI

with a bulgur wheat & couscous filling

SERVES 4

Fiddly? Tick. Worth it? Absolutely. OK, so you're probably not going to make this often but that's fine, because there's a place for special dishes in our repertoire too – I sometimes earmark this one for a Sunday when I have a bit more time. The good news is that you can make the involtini in advance and refrigerate them until needed (just be sure not to add the sauce until you're just about to bake this dish, otherwise it will be absorbed into the rolls). I always think this impressively rustic dish looks like it was made with love, which is never a bad thing when you're feeding friends.

3 tablespoons olive oil

2 large aubergines, cut lengthways into
   1 cm thick slices

sea salt flakes and black pepper

small bunch of fresh basil, finely chopped

small bunch of flat leaf parsley, finely
   chopped

sea salt flakes and black pepper

Bulgur wheat & couscous filling

100g bulgur wheat

100g couscous

1 heaped teaspoon ground cumin

1 teaspoon fine sea salt flakes

about 200ml boiling water

juice of 1 lemon

50g toasted pine nuts

50g sultanas or raisins

Spicy tomato sauce

1 tablespoon olive oil

3 garlic cloves, minced

200g canned tomatoes

200ml passata (sieved tomatoes)

150ml water

1 teaspoon chilli powder

1 tablespoon maple syrup

sea salt flakes and black pepper

1. Preheat the oven to 220°C (200°C fan), Gas Mark 7.

2. For the tomato sauce, heat the olive oil in a large saucepan over a medium heat, add the garlic and sauté for 2–3 minutes, or until aromatic. Add the tomatoes, passata and measured water and stir to combine, breaking up any large pieces of tomato with the back of a spoon. Stir in the chilli powder and maple syrup, season generously and simmer for 30–40 minutes until the sauce is thick and glossy, then remove from the heat and set aside.

3. Meanwhile, set a griddle pan over a medium–high heat and lightly brush with a little olive oil. Brush the aubergine slices with a little more oil and griddle in batches for 3–4 minutes on each side until charred and marked. Transfer to a dish, season lightly and set aside to cool.

4. For the filling, place the bulgur wheat, couscous, cumin and salt in a large mixing bowl and toss to combine. Pour enough boiling water over the grains to just cover, then cover with clingfilm or a plate. Set aside for 15–20 minutes, until the water has been completely absorbed, before fluffing up with a fork and stirring through the lemon juice, pine nuts, sultanas and herbs. Check for seasoning.

5. Ladle a third of the sauce over the bottom of a 30 x 20cm baking dish. Take a slice of griddled aubergine and place a spoonful of the bulgur wheat filling in the centre at the widest part, then carefully roll it up to form a neat little bundle. Transfer to the baking dish and repeat until all the aubergine slices have been filled (you can serve any leftover filling alongside the dish or keep it for a lunch).

6. Spoon the remaining sauce evenly over the involtini, cover with foil and bake for 25 minutes before removing the foil and returning to the oven for a further 15 minutes until lightly golden and bubbling. Remove from the oven and leave to cool slightly before serving alongside a crisp green salad.

MIXED PEPPER CAPONATA

with capers & popped quinoa

SERVES 2-4

If I had to pick one salad to eat for the entirety of the summer then this is the one I would choose. In truth, I've been making variations on caponata for years now and I'm not even close to tiring of it. It's often the one dish I will bring to a barbecue because it requires the least explaining and has a way of covering most dietary requirements – dairy-free, gluten-free, you name it. There's something uniquely wonderful that happens to a pepper when roasted – in fact, I'm not sure there's a greater vegetable transformation to be found. Never have I come across such a universally pleasing dish – not even the remnants of the dressing are safe, just you wait and see. It's no wonder it's become a crucial part of my recipe armour, and I really hope it'll become part of yours, too.

1 large red pepper, cored, deseeded and cut into quarters

1 large green pepper, cored, deseeded and cut into quarters

1 large yellow pepper, cored, deseeded and cut into quarters

30g quinoa (any colour or a mixture), rinsed and dried

1 teaspoon baby capers

Dressing

large handful fresh basil

1 large garlic clove

2 teaspoons baby capers

pinch of sea salt flakes

3 tablespoons balsamic vinegar

2 tablespoons extra virgin olive oil

juice of ½ lemon

½ tablespoon agave nectar (or maple syrup or brown sugar)

black pepper

1. Preheat a grill to high.
2. Arrange the pepper quarters skin-side up on a baking sheet, place under the hot grill and cook for 8–10 minutes, or until the skins are black and blistered. Transfer to a bowl, wrap in clingfilm and leave to cool, then peel the skins off and cut the flesh into thick ribbons. Transfer to a shallow serving dish.
3. Heat a cast-iron frying pan with a lid until it begins to smoke. Tip the quinoa into the pan, turn the heat down to medium and cover with the lid. Cook for 1–2 minutes, shaking the pan as you go and checking on the quinoa from time to time to ensure it isn't burning, until the quinoa has popped. Remove from the heat and transfer to a baking sheet to cool.
4. For the dressing, place the basil, garlic, capers and salt in a pestle and mortar and grind to a rough paste. Add the balsamic vinegar, oil, lemon juice and agave nectar, season generously and mix together vigorously until it emulsifies.
5. Drizzle the dressing over the peppers and scatter over the popped quinoa and capers. Serve.

WASABI-DUSTED POPCORN

SERVES 4–6

Popcorn is my perennial snack of choice. Granted, my husband is the designated 'popper' while I am the 'coater' – that is, he does all the hard work and I get to pretty it up at the end. Story of my (or should I say his) life. My current flavour kick is a combination of coconut butter (yes, coconut oil will do at a pinch) and a generous dusting of palm sugar, wasabi and salt in almost equal proportions. The oven stage is optional but I feel that having been coated with butter and/or oil, the once-crisp popcorn needs to regain its form again, so it's worth the extra effort.

1 teaspoon wasabi powder

1 tablespoon palm sugar

½ teaspoon pink Himalayan salt

1 teaspoon coconut oil

100g popcorn kernels

50g coconut butter

1. Preheat the oven to 200°C (180°C fan), Gas Mark 6. Line a baking sheet with baking paper.
2. Combine the wasabi powder, palm sugar and salt in a bowl and set aside until needed.
3. Heat the coconut oil in a large heavy-based saucepan over a medium–high heat. Add a couple of popcorn kernels initially to test the temperature – as soon as they begin to pop, add the remaining kernels and clamp on the lid. Once the kernels begin to pop more vigorously, shake the pan to ensure they all reach the heat evenly, and when the popping slows to just a few pops here and there, it's time to take the pan off the heat and tip the popcorn into a bowl.
4. Meanwhile, gently melt the coconut butter a little in a separate saucepan (it doesn't need to be completely liquefied, as the hot popcorn will melt it further). If it starts to brown a little, simply take it off the heat and give it a good stir.
5. Pour the coconut butter over the popcorn along with half the wasabi powder mixture and mix it together with a wooden spoon or spatula, ensuring all the kernels are coated.
6. Transfer the popcorn to the prepared baking sheet, sprinkle over the remaining wasabi powder mixture and stir to combine, then pop in the oven for 8–10 minutes until crunchy and golden. Remove from the oven and set aside to cool before serving. Any leftover popcorn will keep stored in an airtight container for up to 3 days.

PEARL BARLEY PAELLA

with paprika-roasted tempeh

SERVES 4

Tempeh isn't something I eat a tremendous amount of although I do favour its inclusion here. Tossed in smoked paprika and a touch of sugar (don't omit it) and roasted until golden (or as golden as tempeh gets), it does have the ability to bring this dish together. I often use pearl barley in place of rice when making paella and I adore its inimitable chew – it might not be authentic but it's certainly damned delicious, so you'll be getting no apologies from me. Served this dish with a glass of chilled wine, I could almost be forgiven for thinking I'm dining on the Costa Brava. Either that or my finely tuned imagination is wreaking havoc with reality again. Probably the latter.

1 tablespoon olive oil
1 onion, finely chopped
1 celery stick, finely chopped
1 carrot, finely chopped
3 garlic cloves, minced
grated zest and juice of ½ lemon
1 teaspoon smoked paprika
220g pearl barley
1 litre vegetable stock
2–3 saffron threads
400g can chopped tomatoes
1 bay leaf
100g green beans, chopped
50g frozen peas

Paprika-roasted tempeh
1 teaspoon smoked paprika
½ teaspoon garlic powder
pinch of brown sugar
3 tablespoons olive oil
150g tempeh, cubed
sea salt flakes and black pepper

To serve
30g sunflower seeds
small handful of flat leaf parsley, roughly
   chopped
1 lemon, cut into wedges

1. Preheat the oven to 220°C (200°C fan), Gas Mark 7.
2. Heat the oil in a large deep frying pan over a medium heat. Add the onion, celery and carrot to the pan, season and sweat for 3–4 minutes, or until the vegetables begin to soften.
3. Add the garlic, lemon zest and paprika to the pan and sauté for 1–2 minutes, or until aromatic. Stir through the pearl barley, add the stock, saffron, tomatoes and bay leaf, bring to a simmer and cook for 50 minutes, stirring occasionally, until the pearl barley grains are tender but still retain some bite.
4. Meanwhile, make the tempeh. Combine the smoked paprika, garlic powder, sugar and oil in a bowl, add the tempeh and toss together. Season with salt and pepper and roast for 25 minutes, or until browned.
5. Add the green beans to the paella and cook for a further 10 minutes, adding the peas a few minutes before the end. Squeeze over the lemon juice and season to taste, then remove from the heat and top with the roasted tempeh pieces. Garnish with sunflower seeds, roughly chopped flat leaf parsley and lemon wedges before serving.

PUY LENTIL RAGU

with homemade tagliatelle

SERVES 4

Everyone and their granny has their own definitive answer to the vegan ragu recipe question. And while I do waiver between red and green lentils, the green win out because they can stand up to more vigorous simmering without dissolving into mush. Perhaps the most satisfying ribbons of loveliness I have ever created, the homemade tagliatelle are worth every second of rolling and re-rolling.

1 tablespoon olive oil
1 red onion, finely chopped
1 carrot, finely chopped
1 celery stick, finely chopped
100g mushrooms, finely chopped
4 garlic cloves, minced
1 heaped teaspoon dried oregano
150g Puy lentils, rinsed and drained
100ml vegan red wine
1 heaped tablespoon tomato purée
400g can chopped tomatoes
150ml passata (sieved tomatoes)

1 tablespoon balsamic vinegar
½ tablespoon yeast extract spread
½ tablespoon brown or palm sugar
400ml water
1 bay leaf
sea salt flakes and black pepper

Pasta
400g '00' pasta flour, plus extra for dusting
1 teaspoon sea salt flakes
250ml water
1 tablespoon olive oil

1. For the pasta, place the flour and salt in a food processor and pulse to combine. Whisk the water and oil together and gradually add to the flour, pulsing continuously, until the mixture forms a rough dough ball. Turn out on to a clean surface and knead for 1 minute, then wrap in clingfilm, transfer to the refrigerator and leave to rest for 1–2 hours.

2. Heat the olive oil in a large frying pan over a medium heat. Add the onion, carrot and celery, season, cover and sweat for 5–7 minutes, until the vegetables begin to soften. Add the mushrooms and cook for a further 2-3 minutes until softened.

3. Add the garlic, oregano and Puy lentils to the pan and cook, stirring, for 1–2 minutes until the aromas begin to exude. Pour in the red wine, increase the heat to high and cook until the wine has evaporated.

4. Stir in the tomato purée, then add the canned tomatoes, passata, balsamic vinegar, yeast extract spread, sugar and measured water. Season generously, add the bay leaf and simmer for at least 1 hour, stirring frequently, until the lentils are cooked and the sauce is thick and glossy.

5. Roll the pasta dough out on a lightly floured work surface until it is almost transparent, turning it frequently so it doesn't stick. Using a sharp knife, cut the dough into tagliatelle-sized strips. (alternatively, use a pasta maker if you have one.) Dust the ribbons with flour to prevent sticking.

6. Bring a large pan of salted water to the boil, add the pasta to the pan and cook for 3–4 minutes until al dente. Drain and divide between warmed bowls, top with the ragu and serve.

SWEET POTATO & WALNUT KOFTAS

MAKES 12

Walnuts are a wonder – and I'm not just talking about their omega-3 content, although I'll admit that is something of a draw. For me, vegan meatballs, burgers and anything else of that ilk can be a little underwhelming, with a tendency to fall apart at first bite. I know you know what I mean. This is where the humble walnut (with a little help from the ever-reliable sweet potato) comes in. Not only do walnuts add bite and texture but, crucially, they help form a surprisingly 'meaty' ball with the added bonus of being, well, good for you. However you shape them, these koftas are guaranteed to be devoured, whether served as finger food at parties (with requisite spicy dip accompaniment), stuffed into pittas loaded with salad, avocado and hummus (standard) or even doused in a rich tomato sauce for a twist on meatballs and spaghetti (my preference, if anyone's asking). Certified winners, whichever way you go.

1 small sweet potato, halved	½ teaspoon ground coriander
2 tablespoons olive oil	¼ teaspoon ground cinnamon
1 tablespoon milled flaxseed	½ teaspoon dried chilli flakes
100g lightly toasted walnuts	small bunch of fresh coriander, roughly
50g panko breadcrumbs	chopped
1 teaspoon dried oregano	1 spring onion, very finely chopped
1 teaspoon ground cumin	sea salt flakes and black pepper

1. Preheat the oven to 220°C (200°C fan), Gas Mark 7.
2. Lightly brush the sweet potato halves with 1 teaspoon of the olive oil, arrange skin-side down on a tray and bake for 40 minutes until soft. Remove from the oven, scoop out the flesh into a bowl and season lightly. Set aside to cool.
3. Combine the flaxseed with 3 tablespoons water. Set aside for 5–10 minutes.
4. Place the walnuts in a processor and pulse to a fine crumb. Add the breadcrumbs, oregano, spices and flaxseed mixture and pulse again to combine. Transfer to a large mixing bowl, add the coriander, spring onion and sweet potato and season generously. Fold to combine, working the sweet potato into the mixture until completely incorporated.
5. Heat the remaining oil in a frying pan over a medium heat.
6. Take a tablespoon of the mixture and gently form it into a cigar-like cylinder using your fingers. Repeat with the remaining mixture, then add the kofta to the pan in batches and fry for 3–4 minutes on each side, or until golden, turning carefully as you go. (Be sure not to overcrowd the pan or the temperature will lower, resulting in the kofta absorbing too much oil.) Transfer to a plate lined with kitchen paper to drain briefly. Serve hot or cold.

HOT AUBERGINE DIP STEW

SERVES 2

Stews are the backbone of my cooking – they bring solace in times of need and comfort in times of contentment. Here the soft aubergine flesh adds real depth and creaminess to what is a pretty basic chickpea stew, but then again, I've never been ashamed of keeping things simple. The tarragon is a must-have addition, bringing an unusual but moreish aniseedy vibe to the dish and giving it some star quality in the process. Obviously cashew cream solves most ills, but in this instance it plays second fiddle to the aubergine – hot in every sense of the word.

1 large aubergine, halved

2 tablespoons olive oil

1 small red onion, roughly chopped

2 garlic cloves, minced

2 tarragon sprigs, finely chopped, plus extra to garnish

¼ teaspoon cayenne pepper

1 courgette, halved lengthways and sliced

2 carrots, halved lengthways and sliced

250ml water

1 vegetable stock cube

300g canned chickpeas, rinsed and drained

250ml Cashew Soured Cream (*see* page 10)

75g raisins

sea salt flakes and black pepper

75g toasted flaked almonds, to garnish

1. Preheat the oven to 220°C (200°C fan), Gas Mark 7.

2. Score the aubergine halves and brush generously with 1 tablespoon of olive oil. Season and place cut-side down on a baking tray, then bake for 25–30 minutes, or until completely soft. Set aside to cool for 5 minutes or so before scooping out the soft flesh and chopping to a fine pulp (don't use the food processor as you want a coarse texture here).

3. Heat the remaining olive oil in a large saucepan over a medium heat, add the onion, season and sweat for 2–3 minutes until slightly softened. Add the garlic, tarragon and cayenne pepper to the pan and sauté for a further 3–4 minutes, until the onion has softened and is almost translucent.

4. Add the courgette and carrot to the pan, season and sauté for 5 minutes, or until softened, then pour over the measured water, add the stock cube and stir to dissolve. Add the chickpeas, bring to a gentle simmer and cook for 15–20 minutes until reduced.

5. Stir in the aubergine pulp and cashew soured cream, season generously with salt and pepper and simmer for a further 10 minutes, adding the raisins right at the end of cooking just to heat through. Divide between plates and sprinkle over the toasted flaked almonds and extra tarragon to garnish. Serve with couscous.

POLENTA 'HYGGE' BOWL

with braised bay lentils & harissa-roasted celeriac

SERVES 4

Hygge is a state of mind, in my opinion, but I try to keep my 'inner cosy' topped up with wholesome bowls like this one. A vastly underrated ingredient, polenta doesn't naturally have a ton of flavour, which ensures it 'perfect backdrop' status, lending its soft yellow hue to more robust accompaniments.

1 litre water

150g spring greens, sliced

2 teaspoons sea salt flakes

100g polenta

juice of ½ lemon

100ml plant milk (*see* page 9)

1 tablespoon extra virgin olive oil

2 tablespoons grated vegan parmesan or nutritional yeast (optional)

black pepper

Lentils

1 tablespoon olive oil

1 carrot, grated

3 garlic cloves, minced

1 heaped teaspoon za'atar, plus extra to garnish

100g green lentils, rinsed and drained

750ml water

1 bay leaf

sea salt flakes and black pepper

Celeriac

1 tablespoon harissa paste

2 tablespoons olive oil

juice of ½ lemon

1 celeriac, peeled and cut into cubes

sea salt flakes and black pepper

1. Preheat the oven to 220°C (200°C fan), Gas Mark 7.
2. For the lentils, heat the olive oil in heavy-based saucepan over a medium heat, add the carrot, season and sauté for 1–2 minutes until slightly softened. Add the garlic and za'atar and sauté for a further 2–3 minutes until aromatic, then stir in the lentils and pour over the measured water. Add the bay leaf, season generously with salt and pepper and bring to the boil, then reduce the heat to a simmer and cook for around 1 hour, or until the lentils are soft and the sauce has thickened. Keep warm.
3. Meanwhile, make the celeriac. Whisk the harissa, oil and lemon juice together in a bowl to combine. Arrange the celeriac pieces in a large baking dish, pour over the harissa mixture and toss to coat, then season and roast for 30 minutes, or until the celeriac is cooked through. Set aside.
4. Bring the measured water to the boil in a saucepan. Add the spring greens to a steamer, set it over the pan and steam for 2–3 minutes, or until wilted. Remove the greens from the steamer and set aside.
5. Add the salt to the water and stir to dissolve, then gradually add the polenta, whisking to avoid any lumps. Reduce the heat to low and cook for 15 minutes, stirring frequently, until just beginning to thicken, then stir in the lemon juice, plant milk, olive oil and parmesan or yeast flakes, if using. Season and cook, stirring, for 1–2 minutes more, then remove from the heat and divide among bowls.
6. To serve, spoon the lentils over the polenta, layer over the spring greens and roasted celeriac and sprinkle over a little extra za'atar to garnish.

TURMERIC & GINGER SWEET POTATO SOUP

with roasted tamari tofu pieces

SERVES 2–4

Fresh turmeric is an obsession of mine. That nubbly little root, boasting a list of medicinal benefits the length of my arm, can basically do no wrong. I pop it in smoothies, oatmeals and stews – although I especially adore it in soups. Sweet potato and turmeric seems to be the perfect pairing, not least because of their similarly vibrant orange interiors (although that may have something to do with it) but mostly due to the extra, essential 'soothe-factor' this root vegetable lends to proceedings. The gorgeous citrus notes of the freshly grated turmeric can't really be replicated by using its more pungent ground cousin but at a pinch a teaspoon of this will still render a pot of pure golden bliss.

1 tablespoon groundnut oil

1 onion, finely chopped

2 large sweet potatoes, peeled and roughly chopped

3 garlic cloves, minced

1 thumb-sized piece of fresh root ginger, peeled and grated

1 thumb-sized piece of turmeric, grated (or 1 scant teaspoon ground turmeric)

1 vegetable stock cube

750ml water, plus extra if necessary

sea salt flakes and black pepper

Roasted tamari tofu

200g firm tofu, cut into 2cm cubes

2 tablespoons soy sauce or tamari

2 tablespoons groundnut oil

½ tablespoon sesame oil

1 tablespoon maple syrup

juice of ½ clementine

To serve

1–2 teaspoons dried chilli flakes

1 tablespoon chopped chives

1. Preheat the oven to 220°C (200°C fan), Gas Mark 7.

2. Heat the groundnut oil in a large saucepan over a medium heat, add the onion and sweat for 2–3 minutes until it begins to soften.

3. Add the sweet potato to the pan along with the garlic, ginger and turmeric and cook, stirring, for a further 2–3 minutes until nicely aromatic. Add the stock cube and measured water and stir to dissolve, then bring to a gentle simmer and cook for 20–25 minutes, or until the sweet potato pieces are nice and soft.

4. Meanwhile make the tofu. Place the tofu in an ovenproof dish. Whisk the rest of the ingredients together in a small bowl until smooth, pour over the tofu pieces and toss to combine. Cover with foil and roast for 20 minutes, then remove the foil and roast for a further 5–10 minutes until golden and glistening. Set aside until needed (the tofu pieces will continue to firm as they cool).

5. Transfer the sweet potato mixture to a blender and blitz until completely smooth, then return to the pan and gently heat through, adding a little extra water if you feel the soup needs thinning out a little.

6. Once heated, divide the soup among bowls and top with the tofu pieces, a sprinkling of chilli flakes and some chopped chives.

BAKED APPLE PIE OATMEAL

SERVES 2–4

Apple pie is one of my favourite desserts. This brunch version was a matter of trial and error, before I decided that the vessel in which it is cooked was the most crucial element. Of course, you can sauté the apples in a saucepan and then construct the 'pie' in an ovenproof dish, but it really doesn't give the same result. Not only does my method save on the washing up, it also means you can serve the baked oatmeal in slices, thus perpetuating the illusion of a regular pie (albeit one you can enjoy first thing).

1 heaped teaspoon coconut oil

4 sweet eating apples, peeled, cored and
   sliced

1 heaped teaspoon ground cinnamon

¼ teaspoon freshly ground nutmeg

3 tablespoons palm sugar

1 tablespoon maple syrup

juice of ½ lemon

pinch of sea salt flakes

250ml water

2–3 tablespoons oat or soy cream, to serve

Oatmeal
100g rolled oats
1 teaspoon ground cinnamon
½ teaspoon ground ginger

¼ teaspoon freshly grated nutmeg

¼ teaspoon allspice

pinch of sea salt flakes

100ml water

150ml almond or other plant milk
   (*see* page 9)

50g toasted hazelnuts

50g sultanas or golden raisins

1 tablespoon maple syrup

20g flaked almonds

Super-quick maple cream
2 tablespoons light tahini
2 tablespoons maple syrup
pinch of sea salt flakes
1–2 tablespoons plant milk (*see* page 9)

1. Preheat the oven to 200°C (180°C fan), Gas Mark 6.

2. For the oatmeal, combine the oats, spices and salt in a large bowl and pour over the measured water and almond milk. Set aside to soak for 10 minutes.

3. Meanwhile, heat the coconut oil in large ovenproof frying pan over a medium–high heat. Add the apples and sauté until they begin to soften and colour, about 8–10 minutes. Sprinkle over the spices and palm sugar and sauté for a further 1–2 minutes, then add the maple syrup, lemon juice and salt. Leave to cook for a few seconds, then pour over the water, increase the heat to high and let the sauce bubble away for 10 minutes, or until it has begun to thicken and form a loose caramel. Remove from the heat.

4. Add the hazelnuts, sultanas and maple syrup to the oatmeal bowl and stir to combine, then spoon the mixture evenly over the apples in the pan, leaving an outer ring of apple pieces visible. Scatter over the flaked almonds and bake for 15 minutes until the apples are bubbling and the oatmeal is golden.

5. Meanwhile, make the maple cream by whisking the tahini, maple syrup and salt together in a bowl, adding a splash or two of plant milk to give it a pourable consistency.

6. Remove the baked oatmeal from the oven and place it in the middle of the table (where it will take centre-stage at any casual brunch). Drizzle over the maple and oat creams and serve.

CHOCO CHAI QUINOA BOWL

SERVES 2

I can't decide if this should be a breakfast dish or a dessert. It feels almost too indulgent to be eaten in the morning, but maybe a bit too virtuous to be considered for afters? You see my quandary. I cook my quinoa before adding it to the chocolate milk mixture, mainly because you don't want the milk to reach boiling point, as it will impair the flavour. The chai spices are the perfect accompaniment to the delicate quinoa, with the fresh cherries offering a welcome nod to summer. For a fun brunch option, fill several small tumblers with the mixture and refrigerate until needed, adding the toppings just before serving. A drizzle of sweetened tahini wouldn't go amiss, either.

125g quinoa (any colour)
500ml water
500ml unsweetened almond milk
2 tablespoons raw cacao powder or cocoa
1 heaped tablespoon maple syrup
pinch of pink Himalayan salt
1 small cinnamon stick
3 cardamom pods
1 star anise

To serve
handful of cherries, halved and pitted
2 tablespoons toasted coconut flakes
30g good-quality plain dark chocolate
    (70% cocoa solids), broken into chunks
½ teaspoon freshly grated nutmeg and/or
    ground cinnamon

1. Add the quinoa to a saucepan and pour over the measured water. Cover with a lid and bring to a boil, then reduce the heat to a simmer and cook for 8–10 minutes, or until all the liquid has been absorbed. Remove from the heat and leave to steam, covered, for 5 minutes, then fluff the quinoa grains up with a fork and set aside (this can be prepared up to a day in advance and kept in a suitable container in the refrigerator until needed).

2. Place the almond milk, cacao, maple syrup and salt in a saucepan and whisk to combine. Add the spices and bring to the boil, then reduce the heat to low and simmer gently for 10 minutes, whisking occasionally.

3. Taste the hot chocolate milk for sweetness, adding a little extra maple syrup if you feel it needs it, then tumble in the quinoa and heat gently for a further 2–3 minutes.

4. Divide among bowls and serve topped with cherries, toasted coconut flakes and a chunk or two of plain dark chocolate, sprinkling over a little freshly grated nutmeg and/or cinnamon to finish.

GET-UP-AND-GO COFFEE SHAKE

SERVES 1–2

A cross between a shake and a smoothie, this morning booster is sure to set you up for the day. I'm crazy about coffee but a pure injection first thing leaves me jittery and even though I'm the furthest thing from a morning person, I prefer not to have a racing heart at 7.30am. I've found that bulking this shake up with banana and oats means I get my caffeine fix without the 'climbing the walls' after-effects. If you're really not a coffee drinker, fear not, this tastes just as brilliant without the espresso – bung it in a 'to-go' cup and you'll be ready to face the world.

1 banana, sliced and frozen

1 x 30ml espresso coffee shot

3 medjool dates, pitted

1 tablespoon date syrup

1 heaped tablespoon almond butter

50g rolled oats

1 heaped teaspoon maca powder

100ml plant milk (*see* page 9 – oat or almond are my preference)

1. Place everything in a blender and blend until completely smooth. Pour into glasses and serve.

TIP: If you don't have a frozen banana to hand, simply use a regular banana and add a few ice-cubes before blending.

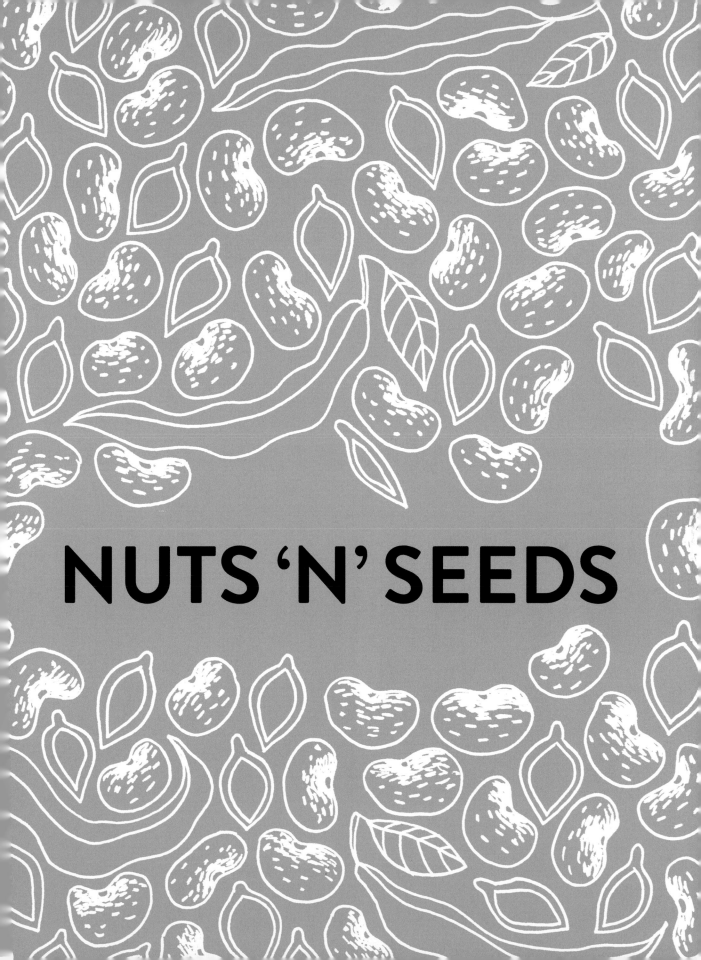

NUTS 'N' SEEDS

CHESTNUT & MISO SOUP

with crunchy chickpea croutons

SERVES 2-4

Chestnuts can be found in abundance over the cold winter months and during that time I try to make as much use of them as I can. Because they blend beautifully they make a terrific base for any festive soup, and the result here is a silky-smooth, earthy offering, perfectly set off by the crunchy chickpea croutons. Make this soup in advance and gently heat it through when needed for an easy starter to any meal or as an elegant stand-alone lunch dish.

1 tablespoon olive oil

1 red onion, finely chopped

1 carrot, finely chopped

1 garlic clove, minced

220g canned or vacuum-packed chestnuts, crumbled

200g canned chickpeas, rinsed and drained

1 heaped tablespoon miso

500ml water, plus extra if necessary

sea salt flakes and black pepper

Chickpea croutons

100g chickpeas, rinsed and drained

juice of ½ orange

2 tablespoons olive oil

1½ teaspoons maple syrup

2 rosemary sprigs, finely chopped

pink Himalayan or fine sea salt flakes

To serve

soy cream

chopped curly parsley

1. Preheat the oven to 220°C (200°C fan), Gas Mark 7.
2. Heat the olive oil in a saucepan over a medium heat. Add the red onion, carrot and garlic to the pan and sauté for 2–3 minutes until starting to soften. Stir in the chestnuts, chickpeas and miso and cover with the measured water. Bring to a gentle simmer and leave to cook for 20 minutes.
3. Meanwhile, make the chickpea croutons. Add the chickpeas to an ovenproof dish and whisk the orange juice, oil and maple syrup together in a bowl to combine. Pour the orange juice mixture over the chickpeas, sprinkle over the chopped rosemary and generously season with salt. Toss to combine and roast for 25–30 minutes, or until golden.
4. Transfer the soup to a blender and blitz until smooth, then return to the pan and heat through, thinning it out with a little extra water if you like.
5. Ladle the soup into warmed bowls or mugs, drizzle over a little soy cream and spoon over the crunchy chickpea croutons. Garnish with a scattering of chopped parsley and serve.

RED THAI CURRIED POTATOES

with a rich macadamia cream

SERVES 2-4

If I had a spirit vegetable it would be the spud. OK, so the potato is actually interchangeable here, because cauliflower (even sweet potato) would work equally well. The curry paste is just the right side of hot, but the unctuous macadamia cream is truly where it's at. I only use two-thirds of it in the recipe, which may seem a tad odd, but I've found that the blender works better when it has more contents to consume. You can keep the remaining cream in the refrigerator for up to 2–3 days and stir it through pasta, add it to casseroles or thin it out to make a sensational salad dressing.

1 heaped teaspoon coconut oil

1 large white onion, sliced

500g salad potatoes, halved

600ml water

1 kaffir lime leaf

sea salt flakes and black pepper

large handful of fresh coriander leaves,
    to serve

Curry paste

4 red chillies

1 lemon grass stalk

4 garlic cloves

1 thumb-sized piece of fresh root ginger, peeled

4 spring onions

juice of 1 lime

½ tablespoon palm sugar

1 heaped teaspoon ground cumin

½ teaspoon ground coriander

2 tablespoons sesame oil

1 teaspoon sea salt flakes

Macadamia cream

100g macadamias, quick-soaked and drained
    (*see* page 8)

150ml filtered water

juice of ½ lime

¼ teaspoon sea salt flakes

1.   To make the curry paste, place all the ingredients into a food processor and blitz for 1–2 minutes until well combined. Set aside until needed.

2.   Heat the coconut oil in a heavy-based saucepan over a medium heat. Add the onion, season lightly and sweat for 5 minutes until translucent.

3.   Add the potatoes to the pan, season and sauté for 2–3 minutes, stirring occasionally to prevent sticking, then pour over the curry paste and stir to coat. Cook for 3–5 minutes to allow the potatoes to absorb the flavours in the pan before covering with the measured water.

4.   Add the lime leaf to the pan, cover with a lid and bring to the boil, then remove the lid and reduce the heat to a simmer. Cook, uncovered and stirring occasionally, for 40 minutes, or until the potatoes are completely cooked through.

5.   For the macadamia cream, place all the ingredients in a blender and blend vigorously, scraping down the sides from time to time, until completely smooth – this may take up to 10 minutes.

6.   Pour two-thirds of the macadamia cream into the sauce and stir to combine, then simmer gently for a further 10 minutes. Season to taste and serve garnished with fresh coriander leaves.

GREEN BEAN SUMMER ROLLS

with a spicy peanut dipping sauce

SERVES 4

Summer rolls are a thing of beauty. Paper thin, they can be filled with just about anything but honestly, it's as if green beans were made to go inside them. They are the perfect length (which saves on chopping), and keeping it an all-green affair just adds to the already uber-fresh vibe of this recipe. Assembling the rolls does take practice and can be time-consuming but when you present a tray of these to guests, their delighted faces will make it all worthwhile.

200g green beans, trimmed
1 thumb-sized piece of fresh root ginger,
    peeled and minced
1 small green chilli, minced
1 garlic clove, minced
1 tablespoon soy sauce or tamari
½ tablespoon rice mirin
½ tablespoon lime juice
pinch of pink Himalayan salt
6 Vietnamese rice paper sheets
30g salad cress
½ fennel bulb, thinly shaved
1 large spring onion, halved and cut into strips
small handful of fresh coriander, roughly torn

Peanut dipping sauce
2 heaped tablespoons crunchy peanut butter
1 heaped teaspoon Sriracha or other chilli
    sauce
1 tablespoon soy sauce or tamari
1 tablespoon rice mirin
juice of ½ lime
2 tablespoons water, plus extra if necessary
pinch of sea salt flakes
½ teaspoon black sesame seeds

1. Bring a small saucepan of salted water to the boil. Add the green beans and lightly blanch for 2–3 minutes. Drain and rinse under cold water, then transfer to a small mixing bowl.

2. Add the ginger, chilli and garlic to the bowl with the beans and mix together, then add the soy sauce, rice mirin, lime juice and salt and toss to combine. Set aside until needed.

3. Fill a large mixing bowl with cold water and plunge one of the rice papers into the bowl. Leave it to soak and soften for up to 1 minute before transferring to a clean tea towel. Carefully reshape the paper so it lies flat before adding your filling.

4. Place a small amount of cress on the half of the soaked paper nearest to you followed by a few green beans and a little fennel, spring onion and coriander. Using wet fingers, fold the edge furthest from you over the filling and tuck in the sides before carefully rolling the paper away from you to form a neat little wrap. Transfer to a plate and repeat the soaking and filling process until all the ingredients have been used.

5. Place all the dressing ingredients except the sesame seeds into a bowl and whisk to combine, adding a little extra water if the dressing is a bit thick. Pour into a serving bowl and sprinkle over the sesame seeds. Serve with the rolls.

CURRIED CHICKPEA & PINE NUT PASTIES

MAKES 4

If a samosa and a Cornish pasty had a lovechild, it would most probably look a little something like this. A happy marriage of pastry and curried chickpea filling, these mini baked wonders are worth the small amount of effort it takes to make them. The key to pastry is handling it as little as possible and making sure not to overwork the mixture: pulse until it just comes together and then wrap it tightly in clingfilm before refrigerating. Avoid the temptation to overfill the pasties, as they may prove difficult to seal. This recipe makes four so if you're serving them at a party (which I heartily recommend) you'll need to double (or maybe even triple) the quantities.

Pastry

100g gram (chickpea) flour
40g strong white flour
large pinch of sea salt flakes
1 teaspoon garam masala
4 tablespoons olive oil
4 tablespoons water, plus extra if necessary

Filling

400g canned chickpeas, rinsed and drained
2 tablespoons pine nuts, toasted
1 spring onion, minced
1 garlic clove, minced
1 chilli, minced
1 thumb-sized piece of fresh root ginger, peeled and minced
1 tablespoon mild curry powder
juice of ½ lemon
1 heaped teaspoon Dijon mustard
small bunch of fresh coriander, finely chopped

1. For the pastry, place the flours, salt and garam masala in a food processor and pulse to combine. With the engine running, gradually add the oil and the water to form a dough, adding an extra splash or two of water if needed.

2. Turn the dough out on to a clean surface and shape into a ball, then wrap in clingfilm and transfer to the refrigerator for 20 minutes to rest.

3. Meanwhile, make the filling. Place the chickpeas in a large mixing bowl and roughly mash. Season generously with salt and pepper, add the rest of the filling ingredients and mix together thoroughly. Season again to taste and set aside until needed.

4. Preheat the oven to 220°C (200°C fan), Gas Mark 7.

5. Turn the dough out on to a floured work surface and divide it into four equal-sized pieces. Shape one of the pieces into a ball, then roll it out into a circular shape to an approximately 5mm thickness. Cut the rolled pastry circle in half.

6. Take a tablespoon of the filling and place it in one corner of the rolled pastry half, leaving enough room around the edges, then fold the pastry over the filling and crimp the edges with a fork to seal. Using your hands, shape the samosa into a rough triangular shape, pinching the corners as you go.

7. Place the pasty on a lined baking tray and repeat the rolling and filling process until all the pastry and filling have been used. Bake for 15 minutes until golden and crispy. Serve hot or cold.

GRIDDLED COBB-STYLE SALAD

with a creamy chive dressing

SERVES 2–4

During my time living in Chicago I developed an appreciation for Cobb salad. Blue cheese usually takes centre-stage, but in this instance (and while there are many convincing vegan alternatives on the market) I've instead enlisted a herby chive dressing, using hummus as the base. I often use hummus in place of cheese – it's particularly wonderful dolloped on pizza and baked. The components of a Cobb salad are typically arranged in neat little rows but because I've opted to griddle the sweetcorn and tomatoes, I prefer to place those around the edges, leaving the raw veggies untouched. The real star of the show is the coconut bacon, which is a bit of a revelation – smoked paprika really is a wonder.

½ teaspoon olive oil

4 small sweetcorn on the cob

150g cherry tomatoes on the vine

1 head of romaine lettuce, roughly torn or chopped

1 cucumber, halved lengthways, seeds removed and sliced

1 ripe avocado, sliced

2 spring onions, sliced

large handful of salad cress

Coconut bacon

70g coconut flakes

2 tablespoons tamari or soy sauce

½ tablespoon balsamic vinegar

½ tablespoon maple syrup

½ teaspoon smoked paprika

Chive dressing

150g hummus

juice of ½ lemon

¼ teaspoon black pepper

small bunch of chives, chopped

1. Preheat the oven to 200°C (180°C fan), Gas Mark 6 and line a baking tray with baking paper.
2. To make the coconut bacon, arrange the coconut flakes on the prepared baking tray in an even layer. Whisk the tamari, balsamic vinegar, maple syrup and paprika together in a bowl, then pour over the flakes and stir to combine. Bake for 8–10 minutes until browned, shaking the pan frequently to prevent burning, then remove from the oven and set aside to cool and firm.
3. Set a large griddle pan over a medium–high heat and lightly brush with the olive oil. Place the corn cobs on the grill and cook for 10–12 minutes, turning as you go, until charred on all sides, adding the tomatoes to the pan halfway through and turning once until also slightly charred and starting to collapse. Remove the corn and the tomatoes from the pan and set aside to cool slightly.
4. For the dressing, put the hummus, lemon juice and pepper in a blender and blitz until smooth. Stir through the chives and set aside.
5. Line the base of a large platter with the romaine lettuce. Arrange the cucumber slices over the lettuce, place the griddled sweetcorn cobs and tomatoes around the edges of the platter and pile the sliced avocado in the centre. Drizzle the dressing over the salad and scatter over the spring onions, coconut bacon and salad cress. Serve immediately.

SWEET POTATO MASH

with pesto-coated cannellini beans

SERVES 2

I affectionately refer to this dish as my 'midweek mania meal', meaning it can be made in a relatively short period of time, is comforting and nourishing in equal measure, and is rather pretty to look at too. Despite it being a three-parter (four if your count the roasted tomatoes), it does feels quite effortless to make. When something tastes this good, who's complaining about a few pots and pans?

1 large sweet potato, peeled and sliced
2 carrots, peeled and sliced
pinch of sea salt flakes
1 teaspoon Dijon mustard
1–2 tablespoons extra virgin olive oil
100g cherry tomatoes on the vine
1 tablespoon olive oil
sea salt flakes and black pepper
1 heaped tablespoon chopped basil leaves,
    to garnish

Pesto
30g basil leaves
30g spinach

2 tablespoons toasted walnuts
juice of ½ lemon
1 small garlic clove
75ml extra virgin olive oil

Beans
½ tablespoon olive oil
1 small white onion, finely chopped
1 garlic clove, finely sliced
400g can cannellini beans, rinsed and
    drained
250ml water
150g roughly chopped spinach
sea salt flakes and black pepper

1. Preheat oven to 220°C (200°C fan), Gas Mark 7.

2. For the pesto, place all the ingredients in a small food processor and blend to form a coarse paste. Season to taste with salt and pepper and refrigerate until needed.

3. Add the sweet potato, carrot and salt to a saucepan, cover with water and bring to the boil. Reduce the heat to a simmer and cook for 15–20 minutes, or until soft. Drain and return to the pan, then season to taste, add the mustard and extra virgin olive oil and roughly mash. Keep warm over a low heat until needed.

4. Place the cherry tomatoes in a baking dish, drizzle over the olive oil and season. Roast for around 15 minutes until soft and slightly charred, then remove from the oven and set aside until needed.

5. For the beans, heat the olive oil in a frying pan over a medium heat, add the onion, season with salt and sweat for 3–4 minutes until translucent. Add the garlic to the pan and sauté gently until aromatic, stirring frequently to ensure it doesn't brown. Add the beans, pesto and measured water and heat gently, then add the spinach, cover with a lid and leave for 2–3 minutes, or until wilted. Season to taste.

6. To serve, divide the mash and beans between bowls. top with the roasted cherry tomatoes and scatter over a little chopped basil to garnish.

MASSAGED KALE & TOASTED WALNUT SALAD

with roasted celeriac & persimmon

SERVES 2–4

I fully realize kale has had its moment, but that doesn't mean it isn't still a wondrous little (or rather large) leaf – fibrous, robust and full of vitamin C. I can't get enough of the stuff and utilize it in just about everything I make, adding it to stews, soups and even salads. When kale is massaged, its tough exterior eventually yields to reveal a softer side – one that can handle a serious dressing and still hold up to a boatload of toppings too. I've gone down the celeriac path here mainly because it's a perennial fave in our house. I like to call it the 'elegant veg' because it has that innate ability to elevate a dish from 'hmmm' to 'aha!' Persimmon (or Sharon fruit, as it's also known) might seem like an odd inclusion but I simply love fruit in salads and now that persimmons make regular appearances in supermarkets, I thought, Why not?

1 celeriac, peeled and cut into 2cm cubes
1 tablespoon rapeseed oil
splash of sesame oil
200g curly kale, tough stalks removed and
    leaves torn
1 large persimmon, cut into rounds
50g toasted walnuts
1 tablespoon chopped chives, to garnish
sea salt flakes and black pepper

Dressing
2 heaped teaspoon wholegrain mustard
juice of ½ orange or 1 clementine
½ tablespoon agave nectar or maple syrup
1 tablespoon soy sauce or tamari

1. Preheat the oven to 220°C (200°C fan), Gas Mark 7.

2. Place the celeriac pieces in an ovenproof dish, pour over the rapeseed and sesame oils, season generously with salt and pepper and toss to combine. Roast for 40 minutes, shaking the dish from time to time, until tender and lightly golden.

3. Meanwhile, place the kale in a large serving bowl. Whisk the dressing ingredients together and pour over the kale, reserving a tablespoon or so for serving. Using your hands, massage the dressing into the leaves for 1–2 minutes until they begin to wilt and soften. Set aside.

4. Once the celeriac is cooked, remove it from the oven and transfer it to the bowl with the kale. Cut the persimmon rounds into quarters and add them to the bowl together with the toasted walnuts. Toss to combine, then drizzle over the remaining dressing and garnish with a few chopped chives. Serve.

CREAMY CURRIED CHICKPEAS

with teriyaki tofu steaks

SERVES 2–4

Midweek meals can often be a struggle. Not wanting to spend an age in the kitchen, we often resort to convenience food or, even worse, a take-away. Thankfully this creamy chickpea curry can be on the table in around 30 minutes, is packed to the rafters with goodness and flavour and (more importantly) satisfies those post-work comfort-food cravings. For the longest time I associated teriyaki with the bottled sort, without realizing the same result could be achieved in minutes at home. A robust, sticky sauce that will convince even the most hardened tofu-phobes among you, this really is a minor plant-based triumph in bean-curd form. I beg you to put your fears aside and give these 'steaks' a whirl before writing this much-maligned ingredient out of your life completely. I have a funny feeling you won't regret it.

½ tablespoon coconut oil

1 red onion, finely chopped

1 thumb-sized piece of fresh root ginger,
     peeled and minced

2 garlic cloves, minced

1 green chilli, minced

230g canned chickpeas, rinsed and drained

1 teaspoon ground turmeric

1 heaped teaspoon garam masala

¼ teaspoon chilli powder

1 heaped teaspoon tomato purée

1–2 tablespoons water

400ml canned coconut milk

1 kaffir lime leaf

½ tablespoon palm sugar

1 heaped teaspoon cornflour

handful of kale

50g golden raisins

sea salt flakes and black pepper

1 tablespoon finely chopped mint, to garnish

cooked basmati rice, to serve

Teriyaki tofu

100ml water

50ml tamari

50ml rice mirin

1 thumb-sized piece of fresh root ginger,
     peeled and minced

1 garlic clove, minced

2 tablespoons agave nectar

1 teaspoon tomato purée

juice of ½ lemon

1 x 400g firm tofu block, pressed (*see* page 11)
     and cut into 4 equal-sized wedges

½ teaspoon olive oil

1.   Heat the coconut oil in a large saucepan over a medium heat. Add the onion, season and sweat for 4–5 minutes until translucent. Add the ginger, garlic and chilli to the pan and cook, stirring, for a further 2–3 minutes until aromatic.

2.   Tumble in the chickpeas and sprinkle over the turmeric, garam masala and chilli powder. Stir to coat, season generously and cook for 2–3 minutes until the spices are nicely toasted. Stir through the tomato purée and loosen with a splash of water, then pour over the coconut milk, add the lime leaf and

palm sugar and season generously. Bring to a simmer, cover with a lid and leave to simmer for
15 minutes.

3.   Meanwhile, for the teriyaki tofu, place all the ingredients except the tofu and oil into a saucepan
and bring to the boil, then reduce to a simmer and cook for 5–10 minutes, or until thickened and
reduced. Take off the heat leave to cool slightly.

4.   Place the tofu wedges in a baking dish. Pour over two-thirds of the teriyaki sauce and brush to coat.

5.   Dissolve the cornflour in a little water and whisk into the curry sauce. Add the kale and raisins and
simmer for a further 10–15 minutes.

6.   Set a griddle pan over a medium–high heat and lightly brush with the oil. Add the tofu wedges and
griddle for 10–12 minutes, turning, until marked on all sides. Remove from the heat and brush over
the remaining teriyaki sauce while they are still warm.

7.   Spoon the curry into warmed bowls, top with the tofu steaks and garnish with some finely chopped
mint. Serve with basmati rice.

CRISPY POTATO CHIPS

with a parsley & almond sauce

SERVES 4

I'm as big a chip fan as the next person but even I need to shake it up now and again. Sliced into rounds and roasted in olive oil, these feel almost like a slightly more voluptuous crisp – although with enough fluffy potato to make them worth your while. Once the potatoes are roasted and golden, up the ante with this parsley and almond sauce. I prefer to keep things a tad on the rustic side, which lends itself rather well to scooping. In my world, these chips and a few cold beers is usually just what the doctor ordered.

350g baking potatoes, cut into 1cm rounds
1 tablespoon olive oil
1 teaspoon dried chilli flakes
1 teaspoon garlic powder
sea salt flakes and black pepper

Sauce
large bunch of flat leaf parsley, leaves and
   stalks
50g flaked almonds
1 sprig rosemary
1 shallot
1 garlic clove
1 tablespoon cider vinegar
juice of ½ lemon
100ml extra virgin olive oil
75ml water, plus extra if necessary

1. Preheat the oven to 220°C (200°C fan), Gas Mark 7. Line a baking tray with baking paper.
2. Arrange the potato rounds on the prepared tray in an even layer, drizzle over the olive oil and sprinkle over the chilli flakes and garlic powder. Season with salt and pepper and roast for 35–40 minutes, or until golden and crispy.
3. Meanwhile, make the sauce. Place all the ingredients in a blender or food processor and pulse to combine, then blend briefly to a coarse pesto-like consistency, adding a little more water if necessary.
4. Transfer the potato chips to a large platter and spoon the parsley sauce over the top. Serve immediately.

COCONUT-CRUSTED POTATOES

SERVES 2-4

On the face of it this is a rather strange (and mildly off-putting) combo. My inner Irish girl is shouting 'no!' while my 21st-century vegan taste buds are saying, 'by golly, this actually works'. The desiccated coconut really does transform into the most delicious coating without any notion of sweetness, giving the humble roast tatty a nifty makeover that would make any dinner guest happy. I often serve these alongside my Celeriac Steaks (*see* page 166) and a decent helping of delicate pea shoots. In a way, this recipe is a weird nod to the queen of glamorous dining, the incomparable Nigella Lawson. Although heaven knows what she'd make of a coconut-encrusted spud.

750g salad potatoes
30g desiccated coconut
3 tablespoons coconut oil
sea salt flakes

1. Preheat the oven to 240°C (220°C fan), Gas Mark 9.
2. Peel the potatoes and halve the slightly larger ones to ensure they are all evenly sized, then place them in a saucepan and season generously with sea salt. Cover with water and bring to the boil, then reduce the heat to a simmer and cook for 10 minutes, or until just starting to cook through.
3. Drain and return the potatoes to the pan and shake it vigorously to roughen up the edges slightly (this will help the potatoes crispen up in the oven), then add the desiccated coconut and toss to coat.
4. Add the coconut oil to a baking tray, transfer to the oven and leave for 4–5 minutes, or until melted and nice and hot. Tumble in the potatoes and toss to coat in the oil (if it's hot enough, they should sizzle and splutter immediately), then roast for 40 minutes until golden and crispy, shaking the pan from time to time.
5. Once cooked, season generously with sea salt and serve.

RED PESTO RISOTTO

with shaved asparagus

SERVES 4

Risotto is the most restorative dish I can think of, and I know that getting a pot of it on the go will soon put my worries at ease. Halfway between a romesco sauce and a regular pesto, this simple red sauce is something special, whether you stir it through risotto, use it as a dip or dollop it over roasted veg. I urge you to keep a batch to hand (it will keep for up to 1 week in the refrigerator). You won't regret it.

200g asparagus spears, trimmed
1 vegetable stock cube
1½ tablespoons olive oil
1 onion, finely chopped
1 celery stick, finely chopped
1 garlic clove, minced
200g arborio rice
juice of ½ lemon
sea salt flakes and black pepper

Pesto
100g blanched almonds
6 sun-dried tomatoes
30g basil
100g cherry tomatoes
1 garlic clove, minced
grated zest and juice of 1 lemon
100ml extra virgin olive oil
sea salt flakes and black pepper

1. To make the pesto, place the almonds in a food processor and pulse until they form a coarse meal. Add the sun-dried tomatoes, basil, cherry tomatoes, garlic, lemon zest and juice and half the olive oil and season generously. Blend again, drizzling in the remaining oil until it forms a rough paste. Transfer to a container and refrigerate until needed.

2. Bring 1.5 litres water to the boil in a saucepan, add the asparagus and blanch for 2–3 minutes, then remove with a slotted spoon and refresh immediately under cold water. Set aside.

3. Add the stock cube to the pan, stir to dissolve and reduce the heat to a very gentle simmer.

4. Heat 1 tablespoon of the olive oil in a heavy-based saucepan over a medium heat. Add the onion, and celery, season and sweat for 5 minutes until translucent. Add the garlic and sauté for 1–2 minutes until aromatic, then add the rice and stir to coat.

5. Add the hot stock to the pan a few ladlefuls at a time until the rice is covered. Bring to a simmer and cook over a medium heat, stirring frequently, until most of the liquid has been absorbed. Continue to cook, stirring and ladling in the stock a little at a time, until the rice is just cooked.

6. Meanwhile, shave the blanched asparagus with a vegetable peeler or slice lengthways into thin strips. Heat the remaining olive oil in a small frying pan or griddle pan over a medium–high heat, add the asparagus strips, season and stir-fry for 1–2 minutes until lightly charred or golden. Squeeze over the lemon juice and remove from the heat.

7. Remove the risotto from the heat and stir through 3 heaped tablespoons of the pesto along with a splash more stock to loosen everything up.

8. Divide the risotto among bowls, topping each with an additional spoonful of the pesto and several strips of the stir-fried asparagus.

DILL-COATED CASHEW CHEESE

with homemade 'nut-pulp' crackers

SERVES 4–6

The one stumbling block that most people encounter when first embarking on or even considering a vegan lifestyle is cheese. I therefore offer up a plant-based solution that might just ease the way. Without getting involved with full-on fermenting, this is the most straightforward vegan cheese you're likely to come across. Investing in a nut milk bag or muslin cloth is essential here, because that is what will help make our 'cheese' as firm as possible. Using this as a base you can add just about anything you like – think of this recipe as a blank canvas and get creative.

Being the thrifty person I am, I cannot contemplate chucking anything away – not even the dregs of nut milk. These crackers were a happy accident, the result of a bid to use up a mountain of the stuff I'd accumulated after a mammoth plant-milk making session (yes, my life really is that exciting). I pretty much always have a batch stored in an airtight jar, ready to be dipped in hummus or to be spread with the above-mentioned creamy 'cheese'. Even my die-hard omnivore friends are obsessed.

200g cashew nuts, soaked and drained
  (*see* page 8)
1 tablespoon coconut oil
grated zest and juice of ½ lemon
1 teaspoon cider vinegar
1 garlic clove (or ¼ teaspoon garlic granules)
2 teaspoons fine sea salt flakes
pinch of white pepper
2 heaped tablespoons nutritional yeast
  (optional)
1 heaped tablespoon finely chopped dill
dried or fresh fruit, to serve

'Nut-pulp' crackers
1 tablespoon milled flaxseed
150g reserved nut milk pulp (*see* page 9)
  or ground almonds
50g spelt flour
½ teaspoon sea salt flakes
50g pumpkin seeds
50g sunflower seeds
1 tablespoon chia seeds
1 tablespoon coconut oil
1 tablespoon agave nectar or maple syrup
50g sesame seeds

1. Add the cashew nuts to a food processor and blitz until reasonably smooth. Add the coconut oil, lemon juice, cider vinegar, garlic, salt, pepper and nutritional yeast, if using, and blitz until completely smooth, scraping down the sides from time to time.

2. Check seasoning, then transfer to a large piece of muslin cloth or a nut milk bag and wrap tightly into a ball. Suspend over a bowl and refrigerate for at least 2–3 hours, or overnight for a firmer texture.

3. Unwrap the cheese ball and use your hands to shape it into your desired form – I like a slightly domed ball.

4. Lightly mix the dill and lemon zest in a bowl, add the cheese and roll to coat evenly. Cover with baking paper, wrap in clingfilm and refrigerate until needed.

5. To make the nut-pulp crackers, preheat the oven to 170°C (150°C fan), Gas Mark 3½. Mix the flaxseed with 3 tablespoons of water and set aside.

6. Place the nut-pulp, spelt flour, salt and the pumpkin, sunflower and chia seeds in a large mixing bowl and mix together with your hands to combine.

7. Melt the coconut oil in a small pan over a low heat and whisk in the agave nectar and 100ml water. Add to the nut-pulp mixture along with the flaxseed solution and incorporate using a spatula.

8. Tip the mixture on to a large piece of baking paper and flatten slightly. Place another piece of baking paper on top and roll or press into as thin a square as possible without it breaking – no more than a 2mm thickness. Carefully remove the top layer of baking paper, trim the edges of the dough and prick all over with a fork.

9. Transfer to a baking sheet, sprinkle over the sesame seeds and bake for 25–30 minutes, or until completely dry but not overcooked. Remove from the oven and leave to cool completely before breaking into shards. Serve alongside the cashew cheese and a selection of dried and/or fresh fruit such as sliced pear or apple.

'GOES-WITH-EVERYTHING' TAHINI SAUCE

MAKES APPROX. 100ML

If ever there was a go-to sauce in my kitchen this is it. Whenever I put a batch on the table at dinner parties or gatherings it is devoured with alarming gusto, usually amid questions of 'but what is it?' I like it reasonably runny but you can add more or less water to suit – it's worth the effort to get the consistency just right, as the sauce is not going to have the same luscious effect if it's too stiff.

3 heaped tablespoons tahini
juice of ½ lemon
¼ teaspoon sea salt flakes

½ tablespoon cider vinegar
½ tablespoon maple syrup
50–75ml water

1. Place the tahini in a bowl, add the lemon juice, salt, vinegar and maple syrup and whisk to combine. Gradually add the water until you achieve your desired consistency (you may not need all of it).

VARIATIONS

> Swap out the lemon for any citrus fruit you fancy – it works particularly well with orange.
> For a more pungent sauce, add some minced garlic.
> For a more fragrant sauce, stir through some chopped fresh herbs.
> For a richer sauce, swap the cider vinegar for balsamic – a splash of pomegranate molasses also works well in this scenario.
> For a sweet sauce, remove the lemon, cider vinegar and salt and replace with the juice of ½ orange. Increase the sweetener content to 2 tablespoons and whisk vigorously together with 50ml water until smooth, then drizzle over freshly baked Pumpkin Muffins (*see* page 235).

SAVOURY FIG & WALNUT STUFFING SLICE

SERVES 8–10

I'm often asked what I eat at Christmas or for Sunday lunch and for the last four-plus years the answer has been something along the lines of this. Similar to a traditional stuffing (although with a bit more to it), this is a reliable recipe that is sure to satisfy. If you can, leave the tin with the mixture in it in the refrigerator overnight before baking – this will result in a firmer texture and make it much easier to cut. While this stuffing slice is terrific with potatoes, gravy and all the trimmings, I look forward to eating it cold in sandwiches, slathered in mustard and served with a few dill pickles. Heaven.

200g stale wholemeal bread
100g toasted walnuts
4 tablespoons olive oil
2 celery sticks, finely diced
3 shallots, finely diced
3 garlic cloves, minced
500g parsnips, grated
150g carrots, grated

1 heaped teaspoon dried oregano
2 heaped teaspoons wholegrain mustard
3 tablespoons dairy-free margarine
6 dried figs, finely chopped
small bunch of flat leaf parsley, finely
    chopped
sea salt flakes and black pepper

1. Place the bread in a food processor and pulse to form fine breadcrumbs. Season generously, add the toasted walnuts and pulse again to combine. Set aside until needed.

2. Heat 1 tablespoon of the olive oil in a large pan over a medium heat. Add the celery, shallots and garlic to the pan, season and sweat for 4–5 minutes until translucent.

3. Add the parsnip, carrot and oregano to the pan, season generously and sauté for 5 minutes until softened. Reduce the heat to low, add the wholegrain mustard, margarine, remaining olive oil and the breadcrumb mixture and stir well to combine, then remove the pan from the heat and stir through the chopped figs and parsley.

4. Spoon the stuffing mixture into a lightly greased 450g loaf tin a little at a time, pressing down firmly with the back of a spoon to compact it nicely. Cover with tin foil and refrigerate overnight (you can cook it straight away but this chilling will result in a firmer slice).

5. When ready to cook, preheat the oven to 220°C (200°C fan), Gas Mark 7.

6. Bake covered for 45 minutes, then remove the foil and bake for a further 10–15 minutes until nicely browned. Remove from the oven and leave to cool in the tin for at least 10 minutes before gently tipping it out on to a serving plate. Cut into slices and serve.

WASABI-ROASTED SPROUTS

SERVES 4

Holler if you love sprouts! Once much maligned, these leafy beauties have officially been given a 21st-century makeover thanks to our current obsession with all things green. As for baby corn – what is this precisely? It always reminds me of that scene from *Big* when Tom Hanks nibbles around the edges of a tiny cob and is left with a limp little stalk. Halved and roasted, however, is definitely where it's at when it comes to these bad boys. Spruced up with a dash of wasabi? Now you're talking.

400g Brussels sprouts, halved lengthways
150g baby corn, halved lengthways

Marinade
1 heaped teaspoon wasabi powder
juice of ½ orange
1 tablespoon soy sauce or tamari
2 tablespoons sesame oil (cold-pressed if possible)
½ tablespoon rice mirin
½ tablespoon maple syrup

To serve
1 heaped tablespoon chopped fresh coriander
1 spring onion, sliced
1 tablespoon sesame seeds
zest of 1 orange
2–3 tablespoons Goes-with-Everything Tahini Sauce (*see* page 151)

1. Preheat the oven to 220°C (200°C fan), Gas Mark 7.
2. Place the sprouts and baby corn in an ovenproof dish.
3. To make the marinade, put all the ingredients in a small bowl and whisk together to combine.
4. Pour the marinade over the veg, toss to combine and bake for 25–30 minutes, giving the pan a little shake from time to time, until tender and lightly golden.
5. Remove the veg from the oven and transfer to a serving dish. Scatter over the coriander, spring onion, sesame seeds and orange zest and finish with a generous drizzle of 'goes-with-everything' tahini sauce, if you like.

FRAGRANT FRIED RICE

with toasted almonds & raisins

SERVES 2–4

If you're seeking a midweek stunner that takes very little prep, this stir-fried rice recipe is just the ticket. I've lost count of the many variations on this super-simple supper I've made over the years, but I always come back to this almond and raisin combo. Crunch and chew are essential components of any vegan dish, in my opinion, and this humble bowl is no exception. This fried rice also makes for a tremendous side dish or you can serve it as part of everyone's current favourite go-to meal, the Buddha bowl. Load it up with tofu and kale and you've got yourself a winner. Fuss-free dining at its best.

200g brown or white basmati rice
½ lemon
1 star anise
1 small cinnamon stick
3 cardamom pods
5 cloves
375ml water
1 tablespoon coconut oil
1 small onion, sliced
1 large carrot, sliced
1 celery stick, sliced

2 tablespoons tamari or soy sauce, plus extra
   to serve
1 thumb-sized piece of fresh root ginger,
   peeled and minced
1 large garlic clove, minced
1 green chilli, seeds removed and minced
1 tablespoon rice wine or cider vinegar
1 heaped tablespoon chopped mint,
1 heaped tablespoon chopped tarragon
50g golden raisins
50g toasted flaked almonds

1. Rinse the rice thoroughly and place in a saucepan with the lemon, star anise, cinnamon, cardamom and cloves. Pour over the measured water, cover with a lid and bring to the boil, then reduce the heat to a simmer and cook for 10 minutes, or until most of the liquid has been absorbed. Remove from the heat and set aside to steam, covered, for 5 minutes before removing the lemon and spices and fluffing up the rice grains with a fork.

2. Heat the coconut oil in a large frying pan or wok over a medium–high heat. Add the onion, carrot and celery and sauté for 4–5 minutes until they begin to soften. Pour over half the tamari, stir in the ginger, garlic and chilli and sauté for a further 3–5 minutes until nicely aromatic.

3. Add the rice to the pan and stir to combine, then pour over the rice wine vinegar and remaining tamari and sauté for a further 5 minutes, or until the rice is heated through and starts to catch slightly on the bottom of the pan.

4. Add the chopped herbs, raisins and almonds to the pan, reserving a little of each for garnish. Stir to combine before spooning on to a large platter or into individual serving bowls. Garnish with the reserved herbs, raisins and toasted almond flakes and serve with extra tamari for drizzling.

STIR-FRIED BROCCOLI

with toasted peanuts

SERVES 2–4

I'm a side-dish fanatic and broccoli is my jam. Don't try to substitute the sprouting variety suggested here with the thicker, more tree-like type, as their long fibrous stems are an integral part of the recipe. And avoid overcooking the broccoli at all costs – you want it just soft but far from floppy. The roasted peanuts bring crucial crunch; I tend to roughly chop them but you could pulverize them using a pestle and mortar, if you prefer. You can also try cashews for a similar result.

75g peanuts
1 tablespoon sesame oil
200g sprouting broccoli
1–2 tablespoons water
1 tablespoon rice mirin
3 tablespoons soy sauce or tamari
½ tablespoon maple syrup
2 spring onions, finely sliced

1. Preheat the oven to 220°C (200°C fan), Gas Mark 7.

2. Arrange the peanuts on a baking tray and toast in the oven for 10–15 minutes until golden, shaking the pan from time. If the peanuts have skins, transfer them to a clean tea towel and rub them vigorously to remove. Roughly chop and set aside until needed.

3. Heat the sesame oil in a large frying pan over a medium–high heat. Add the broccoli and stir-fry for 3–4 minutes until just beginning to colour. Add the measured water, cover with a lid and leave to steam for 2–3 minutes, or until the broccoli has softened.

4. Remove the lid, add the rice mirin, soy sauce and maple syrup to the pan and stir-fry for 2–3 minutes, or until the liquid has reduced to a glossy sauce.

5. Add the sliced spring onion and toasted peanuts and cook, tossing to combine, for a further 1–2 minutes. Serve.

BAKED POTATO NACHOS

with saucy black beans & avocado crema

SERVES 2-4

This is my kind of food. Easy to assemble but packed to the rafters with flavour, it's a veritable smorgasbord for the senses. The halved potatoes take virtually no time to cook and require minimal input – for what might look like a long list of ingredients, you'll be amazed at how easily this whole dish comes together.

2 small baking potatoes, halved and scored
2 small sweet potatoes, halved
1 tablespoon olive oil
sea salt flakes and black pepper

Avocado crema
1 ripe avocado
150ml coconut or soy yogurt
juice of ½ lemon
1 garlic clove, minced
sea salt flakes

To serve
1 spring onion, sliced
1 x Quick-pickled Red Onions (*see* page 184)
small handful of coriander leaves, torn

Black beans
1 tablespoon olive oil
1 small red onion, finely chopped
3 garlic cloves, minced
1 teaspoon dried oregano
1 teaspoon ground cumin
½ teaspoon ground coriander
¼ teaspoon cinnamon
1 teaspoon dried chilli flakes
380g canned black beans in their liquid
1 tablespoon balsamic vinegar
sea salt flakes and black pepper

1. Preheat the oven to 220°C (200°C fan), Gas Mark 7. Line a baking tray with baking paper.
2. Brush the potato and sweet potato halves with the oil, season with salt and pepper and bake for 30–40 minutes, or until cooked through.
3. Meanwhile, make the black beans. Heat the olive oil in a large frying pan over a medium heat. Add the onion to the pan, season and sweat for 4–5 minutes until translucent. Add the garlic and oregano and sauté for 1–2 minutes until aromatic, then add the spices and fry gently for several seconds before adding the black beans in their liquid. Season generously with salt and pepper, stir in the balsamic vinegar and simmer for 20 minutes until the sauce has thickened and reduced. Mash the beans lightly, leaving some beans whole, remove from the heat and set aside.
4. For the avocado crema, mash the avocado and transfer to a bowl along with the yogurt, lemon juice and garlic. Season with salt and stir to combine.
5. Remove the potatoes from the oven and arrange on a large platter. Spoon over the black beans, top with the avocado crema and garnish with the spring onion, pickled red onion and coriander leaves.

EARTHY

QUINOA & CANNELLINI BEAN SOUP

SERVES 4

The inspiration for this dish came via the internet, specifically a travel diary of sorts on YouTube. The video followed a fabulously hippy vegan's exploits in Peru. In a snippet of no more than 5 seconds in length, she was served a bowl of soup in a magnificently ramshackle establishment of the kind that you just know serves the best food. All I could think was that I'd be willing to fly halfway around the world to sample that exact bowl of plant-based awesomeness, but then reality kicked in and I realized I'd have to make do with creating my own. I watched that same 'blink and you'll miss it' shot on repeat, until I was satisfied I'd got the gist of the dish. Of course, I can't be sure about the seasonings used, but by golly if this is not the most comforting bowl of goodness ever to pass my lips. And in deference to the place that inspired it and the hippy who led me to it, I vow to make that voyage to Peru one day.

1 tablespoon rapeseed oil

1 large spring onion, chopped

1 celery stick, chopped

1 green pepper, cored, deseeded and diced

1 small green chilli, minced

3 garlic cloves, finely sliced

small bunch of fresh coriander, leaves
stripped and stalks minced

300g salad potatoes, cut into 1cm rounds

100g quinoa (any colour), rinsed

1 litre water

1 vegetable stock cube

230g canned cannellini beans, rinsed and
drained

sea salt flakes and black pepper

50g lightly salted tortilla chips, to garnish

1. Heat the rapeseed oil in a heavy-based saucepan over a medium heat. Add the spring onion, celery and pepper, season and sweat for 2–3 minutes until starting to soften.

2. Add the chilli, garlic and coriander stalks to the pan and sauté gently until aromatic, about 2–3 minutes. Add the potato and quinoa to the pan and stir to combine, then pour over the measured water and stock cube and stir to dissolve. Bring to a gentle simmer, cover with a lid and cook for around 30 minutes, or until the potato and quinoa are completely cooked.

3. Add the cannellini beans to the pan, season and cook for a further 5–10 minutes, or until the beans are warmed through. Divide the soup among heated bowls and garnish with the coriander leaves and a few lightly salted tortilla chips.

GARLICKY PAN-FRIED MUSHROOMS

SERVES 2

Simple food is where my heart truly lies. Minimizing ingredients and effort while maximizing flavour has become something of an obsession. These garlicky mixed mushrooms are an ideal brunch or quick lunch idea (and are particularly wonderful when served with my favourite Easy Wheaten Loaf, *see* page 224) and can be whipped up in mere minutes – my kind of cooking. For an extra fancy touch, stir through some tangy cashew soured cream or even a dollop of yogurt, as well as a handful of quickly wilted spinach or rocket. This is what I call no fuss, no drama, just easy plant-based food.

1 tablespoon coconut oil

1 large shallot, sliced

1 rosemary or thyme sprig, leaves stripped
   and roughly chopped

400g mixed mushrooms, trimmed and
   roughly torn

juice of ½ lemon

3 garlic cloves, minced

100g spinach

3 tablespoons Cashew Soured Cream
   (*see* page 10)

sea salt flakes and black pepper

freshly toasted Wheaten Bread (*see* page
   224), to serve

1. Heat the coconut oil in a large frying pan over a medium heat. Add the shallot, season and sweat for 2–3 minutes until translucent.

2. Stir in the chopped rosemary and cook for 1–2 minutes, then add the mushrooms and a squeeze of lemon juice. Increase the heat to medium–high and sauté for 5–7 minutes, until the mushrooms begin to colour and reduce.

3. Add the garlic and remaining lemon juice to the pan and cook, stirring, for 3–4 minutes, or until nicely aromatic. Add the spinach and cook, stirring, until gently wilted, then stir through the cashew soured cream.

4. Check for seasoning and serve on top of freshly toasted wheaten bread.

TLT SOURDOUGH SANDWICH

SERVES 2

Tofu bacon is having a bit of a moment and rightly so. Tofu (and tempeh) lends itself brilliantly to this intoxicatingly pungent marinade, with the result being far from anything you'd expect from 'bland' bean curd. It continues to firm up when cooling, so don't be tempted to over-bake it even if it initially feels a little soft to the touch. I normally set it aside for a few minutes before serving, although quite honestly I prefer it cold – it is a snack in itself (keep extras in an airtight container in the refrigerator for up to 1 week), and I have used it in everything from salads to sushi. It might just be my new favourite thing.

2 tablespoons egg-free mayo
4 sourdough bread slices
2 teaspoons Dijon mustard
1 little gem lettuce, leaves separated
1 beef tomato, sliced
sea salt flakes and black pepper
2 dill pickles, to serve

Tofu bacon
1 x 350g firm tofu or tempeh block, pressed
    (*see* page 11)
1 tablespoon tomato purée
2 tablespoons soy sauce or tamari
1 tablespoon balsamic vinegar
1 teaspoon smoked paprika
1 tablespoon maple syrup
½ tablespoon black treacle
1 tablespoon melted coconut oil (or other
    vegetable oil)
1–2 tablespoons water

1. Preheat the oven to 220°C (200°C fan), Gas Mark 7.
2. For the tofu bacon, cut the tofu block into 5mm slices (or slightly thicker if using tempeh). Place the rest of the bacon ingredients in a shallow bowl and vigorously whisk to combine, then dip each tofu slice into the marinade to coat evenly. Transfer to a baking sheet and bake for 25–30 minutes, turning halfway through cooking, until nicely browned and firm. Remove from the oven and leave for 5 minutes to cool and firm further.
3. Spread a little mayo over one slice of sourdough bread and a little Dijon mustard over another. Layer the lettuce and tomato over one of the slices and season with salt and pepper, then top with a few slices of the tofu bacon and a final, generous smear of mayo before sandwiching the slices together. Cut diagonally and serve with a few dill pickles.

CELERIAC STEAKS

with a mushroom stroganoff sauce

SERVES 4

Celeriac steaks are something of a stunner. Not only do they slice beautifully but they also cook in no time, meaning that dinner can be on the table in 30 minutes. The creamy stroganoff sauce is a simple but beautiful accompaniment, and could easily be served alongside rice for a bowl-food type scenario if you prefer. For me though, the star of the show is the roasted celeriac, which has solved many a weeknight dinner dilemma in our house, as well as becoming a bit of a last-minute dinner party staple.

1 large celeriac, peeled and cut into 4 slices, each 2.5cm thick
1 tablespoon olive oil
sea salt flakes and black pepper
1 heaped tablespoon chopped chives, to garnish

Stroganoff sauce
1 tablespoon olive oil
1 leek, trimmed, cleaned and finely chopped
500g chestnut mushrooms, trimmed and sliced
2 garlic cloves, minced
grated zest and juice of 1 lemon
pinch of cayenne pepper
250ml soy, oat or other plant cream
1 teaspoon Dijon mustard
sea salt flakes and black pepper

1. Preheat the oven to 240°C (220°C fan), Gas Mark 9. Line a baking sheet with baking paper.

2. Brush the celeriac slices with the olive oil, season generously and place on the prepared sheet. Roast for 20 minutes, then turn and cook for a further 10–15 minutes, or until nicely browned around the edges. Remove from the oven and set aside.

3. For the stroganoff sauce, heat the olive oil in a large frying pan over a medium heat. Add the leek, season and sweat for 2–3 minutes until softened.

4. Add the mushrooms to the pan, season generously and stir to combine. Cook for 5 minutes, without stirring, until just beginning to colour, then add the garlic, lemon zest, cayenne pepper and 1 tablespoon of the lemon juice. Season with salt and pepper and cook for a further 5–10 minutes until the mushrooms have shrunk and are lightly golden.

5. Pour over the soy cream, stir in the Dijon and remaining lemon juice and bring to a gentle simmer. Cook, stirring, for 1–2 minutes, thinning out the sauce with a splash of water if it becomes too thick. Season to taste.

6. Divide the celeriac steaks among plates and top each with a spoonful or two of the stroganoff sauce. Garnish with a sprinkling of chopped chives and serve with a fresh pea shoot salad.

EASY FLATBREAD SARNIES FROM SCRATCH

MAKES 6–8 FLATBREADS

Flatbreads are a super lunchtime option. The dough itself requires very little attention and the toppings are as flexible as you please. I'm hooked on this red pepper and white bean duo but mashed avocado works just as well. I also like to serve these sandwiches at casual gatherings; simply arrange them on a large plate or platter and let everyone help themselves. Alternatively, you could lay out a selection of different toppings and let them create their own – interactive dining at its best.

200g spelt flour
½ teaspoon fast-action dried yeast
½ teaspoon baking powder
¼ teaspoon sea salt flakes
1 tablespoon poppy seeds
200ml warm water
½ tablespoon agave nectar or maple syrup
1½ tablespoons coconut oil, melted
2 heaped tablespoons pumpkin seeds,
   to garnish

Smoky sautéed pepper strips
1 heaped teaspoon coconut oil
1 large red pepper, cored, deseeded and sliced

1 teaspoon smoked paprika
½ teaspoon za'atar
sea salt flakes and black pepper

Easy white bean spread
300g canned cannellini beans, rinsed and
   drained
1 tablespoon tahini
1 garlic clove, minced
grated zest and juice of ½ lemon
small bunch of fresh coriander
3 tablespoons extra virgin olive oil

1. In a large mixing bowl, combine the spelt flour, yeast, baking powder, salt and poppy seeds.

2. In a separate bowl, whisk together the measured water, agave nectar and 1 tablespoon of the coconut oil to combine. Make a well in the centre of the flour and pour over the liquid, using a fork to gradually work the flour into the liquid in a clockwise motion until it forms a sticky dough.

3. Tip the dough on to a clean, floured surface and knead for up to 10 minutes, adding a little more flour if necessary, until smooth and elastic. Rub the dough in the remaining melted coconut oil, return to the mixing bowl, cover with a clean tea towel and set aside for 10 minutes to rest.

4. Meanwhile, prepare the red pepper. Heat the coconut oil in a frying pan over a medium heat. Add the pepper and season lightly, then sprinkle over the smoked paprika and za'atar and sauté for 5 minutes until softened. Set aside until needed.

5. For the white bean spread, place all the ingredients in a food processor and blend until smooth.

6. Wipe the frying pan clean, turn the heat up to high and heat until smoking. Divide the dough into 6–8 equal sized pieces and shape and roll each into rough, circular pizza-style pittas. Add the breads to the pan one at a time and cook for 3–4 minutes until they begin to puff up, then flip and cook for a further 1–2 minutes until puffed and lightly charred.

7. Spread the flatbreads with the white bean spread, layer over the smoky sautéed pepper strips and scatter over a few pumpkin seeds to finish.

BELUGA LENTIL & BLACK OLIVE DIP

SERVES 4

Dips are an essential part of most cooks' repertoires and while I probably lean on hummus (the original and best) a little too much, I do occasionally venture outside my comfort zone. I adore the rustic brown hue of this lentil offering and even more so the earthy olive overtones that make it a perfect pairing for a slice of fresh crusty white bread and a glass of red wine. Heaven. Almost akin to a paté, this dip would make an excellent starter divided into smaller pots or you could serve it up in one large shallow bowl as part of a casual gathering, finished with a slick of good-quality olive oil and a smattering of pickled peppercorns and my perennial favourite, capers. If you're also stuck in a bit of a hummus rut, may I suggest a trip down lentil lane?

250g pre-cooked beluga lentils
100g cashew nuts, soaked and drained
   (*see* page 8)
1 garlic clove, minced
2 heaped tablespoons chopped black olives
juice of ½ lemon
1–2 tablespoons water
50ml extra virgin olive oil
sea salt flakes and black pepper

To serve
1 tablespoon chopped black olives
1 teaspoon baby capers
½ teaspoon pickled peppercorns, roughly
   chopped
1 tablespoon extra virgin olive oil

1. Place the lentils, cashew nuts, garlic, olives, lemon juice and water in a food processor. Season generously and blend together, gradually drizzling in the olive oil as you go, until the mixture is thick and smooth with no lumps remaining.
2. Season to taste. Serve immediately, or refrigerate until needed – the dip will keep for up to 3–4 days in an airtight container – garnishing with a few finely chopped black olives, a smattering of capers, some pickled peppercorns and a generous drizzle of extra virgin olive oil.

RUSTIC LEEK, POTATO & ARTICHOKE GALETTE

SERVES 4-6

Galettes are essentially fuss-free pies that actually benefit from looking a little rough around the edges. The tattier the better when it comes to encasing whatever filling you choose – I've opted for classic potato and leek, as well as some pre-cooked artichokes for good measure. This rustic delight makes for a sensational centrepiece and I often serve it as part of a Sunday lunch. It's so satisfying no one will be leaving the table hungry…and if you do happen to have leftovers, it's particularly good eaten cold too.

2 large potatoes, quartered
1 heaped teaspoon coconut oil
3 leeks, trimmed, cleaned, halved
   lengthways and sliced
100g artichokes in oil, sliced
1–2 teaspoons olive oil
sea salt flakes and black pepper
large handful of dill, chopped, to garnish

Pastry
200g plain or spelt flour
100g dairy-free margarine or vegetable
   shortening
pinch of fine sea salt flakes
¼ teaspoon brown sugar
2–3 tablespoons ice-cold water

1. Preheat the oven to 240°C (220°C fan), Gas Mark 9.

2. For the pastry, place the flour, margarine, salt and sugar in a large mixing bowl or food processor and lightly rub or pulse together to form a breadcrumb-like mixture. Add the water a tablespoon at a time and work or pulse together to form a dough (being careful not to overwork it at this point). Roll the dough into a ball, wrap it tightly in clingfilm and refrigerate for up to 30 minutes.

3. Meanwhile, add the potatoes to the pan, cover with water and season generously with salt. Bring to the boil, then reduce the heat and simmer gently for 15–20 minutes, or until cooked through. Drain and set aside to cool, then cut into 1cm slices and season.

4. Heat the coconut oil in a small frying pan over a medium heat, add the leeks and sweat lightly for 3–4 minutes until softened. Season and set aside.

5. Remove the pastry from the refrigerator and roll it out on a lightly floured work surface to a 5mm thickness.

6. Transfer the rolled pastry to a lightly floured baking sheet and arrange the leeks in the centre, leaving a 5–7cm border around the edges. Layer over the potato slices and artichokes and drizzle over a little olive oil. Gently fold the pastry inwards to secure the filling and bake for 30 minutes, turning the tray halfway through to ensure an even bake.

7. Remove from the oven and leave to cool slightly, then slice and scatter over a little chopped dill to garnish. Serve.

PAN-FRIED RED CABBAGE

with a herby tofu mayo

SERVES 4

I can't say silken tofu is a mainstay in my kitchen but that doesn't mean it doesn't have its uses. The herby tofu mayo is one such triumph that is so unnervingly like the real thing, it even has me second-guessing. Served alongside the pan-fried cabbage, it's a seriously rich side dish that really packs a punch on the both the texture and flavour front. I like to keep the red cabbage on the crunchier side but if you prefer it slightly more tender, then clamp on a lid during the cooking time to let it steam and soften. Don't scrimp on the mayo however – the bigger the dollop the better.

1 tablespoon olive oil
1 small red cabbage, roughly chopped
1 garlic clove, finely sliced
grated zest and juice of 1 lemon
5–6 radishes, sliced
2 tablespoons toasted pumpkin seeds
sea salt flakes and black pepper

Herby tofu mayo
300g silken tofu
1 heaped teaspoon coconut oil, melted
juice of ½ lemon
1 garlic clove, minced
1 teaspoon Dijon mustard
1 teaspoon agave nectar or maple syrup
¼ teaspoon sea salt flakes
1 heaped tablespoon chopped chives

1.   To make the herby mayo, place the tofu, coconut oil, lemon juice, garlic, Dijon mustard, agave nectar and salt in a blender and blend until completely smooth. Season to taste, then transfer to a bowl, stir through the chives and refrigerate until needed.

2.   Heat the olive oil in a large frying pan over a medium–high heat. Add the cabbage and garlic to the pan, season generously and stir-fry for 10–12 minutes or until it begins to soften.

3.   Squeeze over the lemon juice and stir through the sliced radish, then remove from the heat and transfer to a serving bowl. Sprinkle over the lemon zest and pumpkin seeds and dollop over the mayo to finish.

FALAFEL-STUFFED MUSHROOMS

with kale & quinoa tabbouleh & a coconut & mint dressing

SERVES 4

I'm always searching for ways to make falafel more interesting. Using it as a stuffing made so much sense and I wasn't disappointed with the result. However, it's the pistachio dust accompaniment that is perhaps the more exciting revelation. I sprinkle it over everything from pasta to avocado toast.

400g canned chickpeas, rinsed and drained, reserving 1 tablespoon of liquid
40g flat leaf parsley
2 garlic cloves
1 spring onion
1 small green chilli
2 tablespoons lemon juice
4 portobello mushrooms, trimmed and stalks removed
2–3 tablespoons olive oil
1 teaspoon ground cumin
½ teaspoon ground coriander
sea salt flakes and black pepper

Kale & quinoa tabbouleh
1 tablespoon olive oil
1 leek, trimmed, cleaned, halved lengthways and sliced
175g quinoa, rinsed
1 bay leaf
grated zest and juice of ½ lemon
100g kale, tough stalks removed and leaves roughly chopped
60g flat leaf parsley
1 tablespoon extra virgin olive oil
pinch of sea salt flakes
pinch of black pepper

Pistachio 'dust'
40g pistachios
10g nutritional yeast
pinch of sea salt flakes

Coconut & mint dressing
3 tablespoons coconut yogurt
1 tablespoon tahini
juice of ½ lemon
pinch of sea salt flakes
1 heaped tablespoon finely chopped mint

1. Preheat the oven to 200°C (180°C fan), Gas Mark 6.

2. To make the pistachio 'dust', place the pistachios, nutritional yeast and salt together in a food processor and pulse together until the mixture resembles dust. Set aside until needed.

3. For the coconut and mint dressing, put the coconut yogurt, tahini, lemon juice and salt in a bowl and mix together until smooth, then stir through the mint. Refrigerate until needed.

4. Put the rinsed chickpeas in a clean tea towel and rub them until the skin comes off (this is optional but it does result in a better falafel mixture). Place the chickpeas, parsley, garlic, spring onion, chilli, lemon juice and reserved chickpea liquid in a food processor and pulse until it forms a rough but spreadable paste. Season with salt to taste.

5. Brush the mushrooms all over with the oil. Season the insides with a little salt and pepper and sprinkle over the ground cumin and coriander. Divide the chickpea mixture between the mushrooms equally and top each with a generous sprinkling of pistachio dust. Bake for 45 minutes until tender and lightly golden.

6. To make the tabbouleh, heat the olive oil in a large frying pan over a medium heat. Add the leek, season and sweat for 2–3 minutes until it begins to soften, then add the quinoa, bay leaf and lemon zest. Pour over 500ml water, cover and bring to the boil, then reduce the heat to a gentle simmer and cook for around 10–12 minutes, or until all the water has been absorbed. Remove from the heat.

7. Add the kale to the pan, then cover and leave for 2–3 minutes, or until the kale is gently wilted. Stir through the parsley, lemon juice, olive oil, salt and pepper.

8. To serve, spoon the warm quinoa tabbouleh on to plates and top with the stuffed mushrooms, adding a dollop of the coconut dressing on the side and a sprinkling of the pistachio 'dust' to finish.

INDIVIDUAL MUSHROOM WELLINGTONS

SERVES 4

Ready-made pastry to the rescue, this time in the form of mushroom Wellingtons – sensational centrepieces for any meal. The trick is to tuck the pastry tightly around the mushroom, making sure there are no air bubbles, so that it shrinks as the mushrooms cooks and reduces. Serve with steamed green beans and a few simply boiled salad potatoes for an elegant supper.

2 tablespoons olive oil

3 shallots, finely chopped

4 large garlic cloves, minced

200g green lentils, rinsed and drained

2 bay leaves

750ml water

1 vegetable stock cube

1½ teaspoons Marmite

4 large portobello mushrooms, trimmed

100g kale, leaves torn and stems removed

juice of ½ lemon

2 sheets of vegan ready-made puff pastry, thawed if frozen

sea salt flakes and black pepper

1. Heat 1 tablespoon of the olive oil in a large saucepan over a medium heat. Add the shallots to the pan, season and sweat for 2–3 minutes until translucent. Stir in the garlic and sauté for 1–2 minutes, then add the lentils, bay leaves, measured water and stock cube. Stir to dissolve the stock cube, bring to a gentle simmer and cook for 40 minutes, or until most of the liquid has been absorbed and the lentils are tender and almost cooked through.

2. Stir the Marmite through the lentils and simmer for a further 5–10 minutes, or until all the liquid has been absorbed. Remove from the heat and leave to cool, then spoon the mixture over the mushrooms. Set the lentil-stuffed mushrooms aside.

3. Heat the remaining olive oil in a frying pan over a medium heat. Add the torn kale, season generously and heat, stirring occasionally, until gently wilted. Squeeze over the lemon juice and set aside to cool.

4. Preheat the oven to 220°C (200°C fan), Gas Mark 7.

5. Roll the pastry sheets out on a floured work surface slightly to enlarge each by about a third, then use a saucer as to template to cut out 8 pastry circles. Cut simple leaf-shaped decorations out of the excess pastry.

6. Place a small heap of kale in the centre of 4 of the pastry circles and lay over the mushrooms, lentil-stuffed side down. Place the remaining pastry circles on top (rolling them out a little more first if you need to for fit) and pinch the sides together with a fork. Trim off any excess pastry and tuck in any gaps as you go, ensuring there are no air bubbles around the mushrooms.

7. Gently press 2 pastry 'leaves' on to each Wellington and bake for 30–35 minutes until golden and crispy. Remove from the oven and leave to cool slightly before serving.

HERBY LENTIL & SAVOY CABBAGE COBBLER

with savoury oaty scones

SERVES 4

Anything that has been topped with mash and then baked is heaven, but I think there's an even more satisfying option out there – the savoury oaty scone. The less you handle the scone mixture the better to ensure a light, crumbly texture. I think Savoy cabbage is such an underused vegetable but in this rather lovely stew it really comes into its own, bringing with it a wonderful texture.

1 tablespoon olive oil	**Scones**
1 leek, trimmed, cleaned and sliced	1 teaspoon cider vinegar
3 garlic cloves, minced	100ml soy milk
220g Puy lentils, rinsed and drained	150g rolled oats
1 vegetable stock cube	1 heaped teaspoon marjoram
1 bay leaf	¼ teaspoon fine sea salt flakes
1 small butternut squash, peeled and chopped	½ tablespoon sugar
1 tablespoon tomato purée	1 teaspoon baking powder
½ Savoy cabbage, roughly sliced	½ teaspoon bicarbonate of soda
150ml soy cream	50g dairy-free margarine
sea salt flakes and black pepper	
1 tablespoon chopped chives, to garnish	

1. Heat the olive oil in a large saucepan over a medium heat. Add the leek, season and sweat for 2–3 minutes until it begins to soften, then add the garlic and cook for a further 1–2 minutes, or until nicely aromatic.

2. Add the lentils, stock cube, bay leaf and 750ml water, bring to a simmer and cook for 10–15 minutes until the lentils have softened and the sauce has reduced slightly, then stir in the butternut squash and tomato purée. Cover and simmer for a further 20 minutes, or until the squash is cooked through.

3. Add the cabbage and cook, covered, for 5–10 minutes, or until wilted. Pour over the soy cream, season and simmer gently for 2–3 minutes, then remove from the heat and set aside until needed.

4. Preheat the oven to 240°C (220°C fan), Gas Mark 9.

5. For the scones, combine the cider vinegar and soy milk in a bowl and set aside for 5–10 minutes to let the mixture curdle.

6. Place the oats in a blender and blitz together to form a fine flour, then transfer to a large mixing bowl. Add the marjoram, salt, sugar, baking powder and bicarbonate of soda and whisk to combine, then work the margarine into the flour using your fingertips until the mixture resembles breadcrumbs. Make a well in the centre and pour over the curdled soy milk mixture, then stir together gently with a metal spoon to form a loose, wet dough.

7. Turn the scone dough out on to a lightly dusted work surface and shape it into a rough ball, then use a dusted rolling pin to roll it out to about a 2cm thickness. Cut the scones out using a 6cm pastry cutter.

Roll the excess into a rough ball and repeat until all or most of the dough is used – you should get about 8 scones from the mixture. Lightly dust the tops with flour.

8. Transfer the stew to a large ovenproof dish and top it with the scones. Bake for 15 minutes, or until the scones have risen slightly and are perfectly crumbly. Sprinkle over the chopped chives and serve.

ROASTED RED ONION & BUTTERNUT SQUASH SALAD

with black quinoa

SERVES 2–4

Warm salads are always welcome in my kitchen. Assembling such dishes is the best part of making them, of course, ensuring that everything is shown off to its perfectly roasted best. The black quinoa can obviously be substituted with the regular (or red) kind but I do have a penchant for the extreme nuttiness of this variety. The sunflower seed dressing is surprisingly cheesy – a quality I sometimes play with by adding a handful of chopped chives before blending.

2 red onions, cut into wedges
1 butternut squash, cut into wedges
1 heaped teaspoon ground cumin
1 teaspoon sumac
1 teaspoon sea salt flakes
1 tablespoon balsamic vinegar
1½ teaspoons pomegranate molasses
2 tablespoons olive oil
175g black quinoa, rinsed and drained
500ml water
150g Savoy cabbage, sliced

juice of ½ lemon
3 dried figs, chopped
black pepper

Sunflower seed dressing
70g sunflower seeds, plus extra to garnish
1 small garlic clove, minced
juice of ½ lemon
¼ teaspoon sea salt flakes
150ml water

1. Preheat the oven to 240°C (200°C fan), Gas Mark 7.
2. Arrange the onion and butternut squash wedges in a large baking dish, sprinkle over the cumin, sumac and salt and toss to combine. Drizzle over the balsamic vinegar, pomegranate molasses and 1 tablespoon of the olive oil and roast for 35–40 minutes, shaking the pan from time to time, until cooked through and golden.
3. Meanwhile, place the quinoa and measured water in a saucepan, cover with a lid and bring to the boil, then reduce the heat to a simmer and cook for 10–15 minutes until the water is completely absorbed. Remove from the heat and set aside to steam, covered, for 2–3 minutes.
4. Heat the remaining 1 tablespoon of olive oil in a frying pan over a medium heat. Add the cabbage, season and gently sauté until it begins to wilt, then add the quinoa and stir to combine. Squeeze over the lemon juice, season generously and stir through the chopped figs. Remove from the heat and set aside until needed.
5. To make the dressing, place all the ingredients in a blender and blitz until completely smooth, scraping down the sides from time to time as you go.
6. Transfer the quinoa to a large platter and distribute the red onion and butternut squash over the top. Drizzle over the dressing and scatter over extra sunflower seeds to garnish.

SWEET POTATO STUFFED SHELLS

SERVES 2–4

If you're after pure unadulterated comfort food then look no further than these stuffed pasta shells. Filled with an incredibly easy sweet potato mixture that mimics all the greatness of a regular mac and cheese, this is a dish I return to so frequently it's become something of a personal classic. I like to retain a little texture by avoiding mashing the sweet potatoes to oblivion – and, perhaps more importantly, ensuring the shells are cooked al dente so as not to turn to mush in the oven. Err on the side of caution and drain the pasta several minutes before the cooking time recommended on the packet for a perfect piping hot pasta bake with the ultimate plant-based twist.

1 tablespoon olive oil

2 leeks, trimmed, cleaned and finely chopped

500g sweet potatoes, peeled, halved and thinly sliced

750ml boiling water

1 vegetable stock cube

150ml soy, oat or coconut cream

juice of ½ lemon

300g conchiglioni (large pasta shells)

1 heaped tablespoon nutritional yeast or vegan parmesan-style cheese

sea salt flakes and black pepper

To serve

1 heaped tablespoon chopped chives

1 tablespoon extra virgin olive oil

1. Preheat the oven to 200°C (180°C fan), Gas Mark 6.
2. Heat the olive oil in a large shallow frying pan over a low heat. Add the leek, season and sweat for 2–3 minutes, or until it begins to soften. Add the sweet potato slices, season and cook, stirring occasionally, for 1-2 minutes, then pour over the boiling water. Add the stock cube and stir to dissolve, then bring to a simmer and cook for 15 minutes, or until the sweet potato is soft.
3. Mash the sweet potato in the pan with a fork or potato masher to form a thick, creamy sauce (it should still have some texture to it, so don't worry if it's not completely smooth). Leave to simmer for a further 10–15 minutes, until slightly thickened and reduced, stirring in the soy cream and squeezing over the lemon juice in the last few minutes of cooking. Season to taste, cover with a lid and remove from the heat.
4. Bring a large saucepan of salted water to the boil, add the pasta shells and cook for 12–15 minutes until not quite al dente, or for just slightly under the recommended cooking time. Drain and leave to cool slightly.
5. Cover the bottom of a baking dish with a layer of the sweet potato sauce. Carefully stuff the pasta shells with the remaining sauce and arrange neatly in the dish, then sprinkle over the nutritional yeast or vegan parmesan and bake for 15–20 minutes until bubbling and golden.
6. Remove from the oven and leave to cool slightly before serving, scattering over some finely chopped chives and a good glug of extra virgin olive oil to finish.

STEAMED BUNS

with shredded hoisin mushrooms & quick-pickled red onions

SERVES 4

There are some dishes I reserve for very special occasions – ones where I know a little impressing is required. And even though there's not a huge amount of effort involved in these steamed buns (enough but not insurmountable), they still retain that air of being a treat. Because they're so innately tactile, they make gatherings go with a bang. The dough can be made ahead of time, wrapped in clingfilm and refrigerated. Unless you happen to have an impressive collection of steaming baskets, you'll probably need to steam them in several batches, although in my opinion the expectation is half the fun.

175ml lukewarm water

1½ teaspoons fast-action dried yeast

1 tablespoon olive oil

1 tablespoon sesame oil

300g plain flour

¼ teaspoon bicarbonate of soda

¼ teaspoon sea salt flakes

2 tablespoons light brown sugar

small handful of fresh coriander, chopped,
    to garnish

Sprouts

200g Brussels sprouts, shredded

pinch of pink Himalayan salt

juice of ½ lemon

½ tablespoon rice mirin

Quick-pickled red onions

1 red onion, finely sliced

1 teaspoon sea salt flakes

1 teaspoon light brown sugar

1 tablespoon rice mirin

1 tablespoon cider vinegar

1 teaspoon black sesame seeds

Shredded hoisin mushrooms

1 tablespoon olive oil

400g chestnut mushrooms, trimmed and
    shredded into thin strips

1 tablespoon soy sauce

½ tablespoon rice mirin

4 tablespoons hoisin sauce

1 tablespoon lemon juice

1. Whisk the measured water and yeast together in a large mixing bowl until frothy. Add the oils and whisk again. Gently combine the flour, bicarbonate of soda, salt and sugar and gradually add to bowl. Mix until it forms a rough dough ball, folding in a little at time. Tip the dough out on to a lightly floured surface and knead for up to 10 minutes, or until the dough is smooth and elastic. Place in a lightly oiled mixing bowl, cover with a tea towel and set aside to rise for 2 hours.

2. For the pickled onions, place the onion in a bowl, cover with boiling water and set aside to soak for 30 minutes. Drain and return to the bowl, then add the salt, sugar, rice mirin and cider vinegar. Stir to coat and set aside to pickle until needed.

3. Put the sprouts in a bowl, sprinkle over the salt, squeeze over the lemon juice and rice mirin and toss to combine. Set aside until needed.

4. For the hoisin mushrooms, heat the olive oil in a frying pan over a medium heat, add the mushrooms and cook, stirring occasionally, until coloured. Add the soy sauce and rice mirin, increase the heat to medium–high and sauté for 1–2 minutes, then add the hoisin and lemon juice and cook for a further 1–2 minutes. Remove from the heat, cover with a lid and set aside until needed.

5. Set a steamer basket over a saucepan one-third full of simmering water.

6. Punch the air out of the risen dough and knead it again for a few seconds, then shape the dough into a ball and divide it into 16 equal-sized pieces. Roll each piece into a ball and then out into a disc, then brush one side of the discs with sesame oil and fold over. Place the folded buns on a small piece of baking paper and transfer them to the steamer, being careful not to overcrowd the basket (you may need to do this in batches). Steam for 6–7 minutes.

7. Sprinkle the black sesame seeds over the pickled red onion.

8. To serve, fill the steamed buns with a spoonful of the hoisin mushrooms and top with the red onion and sprouts. Garnish with some fresh coriander and devour.

SWEETLY
DOES IT

HASSELBACK APPLES

with a coconut caramel sauce

SERVES 6–8

These apples are too cute for words. If you're after an impressive dessert that is seriously simple to make, this is it. Yes, it's just an apple, but it's a perfectly soft and sweet one. Truthfully the wow factor is all down to the caramel sauce, which is something of a game changer. I must admit that prior to this I was something of a palm-sugar-phobe, as I felt it was a bit of a con – sugar is sugar, and all that. However, after experimenting with various different sugars in a bid to bring you the ultimate vegan caramel (it's a tough job), I'm a total convert. Don't panic if you can't get your hands on any though, the caramel works equally well with soft brown sugar, although it won't quite have that depth of flavour the palm variety brings to the table. I now keep a batch of this sauce in my refrigerator at all times and slather it on everything from toast to ice cream…and it's also pretty wonderful straight off the spoon.

4 large apples, peeled, cored and halved

¼ teaspoon freshly grated nutmeg

½ teaspoon ground cinnamon

½ tablespoon coconut oil, plus extra
   for brushing

1 tablespoon maple syrup

30g toasted walnuts, crushed

Coconut caramel sauce

90g coconut palm sugar

125ml water

125ml canned coconut milk (or cream)

1 teaspoon vanilla extract

pinch of sea salt flakes

1. Preheat the oven to 200°C (180°C fan), Gas Mark 6 and brush the bottom of a large ovenproof dish with a little coconut oil.

2. For the sauce, place the coconut palm sugar and water in a saucepan, bring to the boil and cook for 5–7 minutes, swilling the pan to move the contents around but not stirring, until the mixture has reduced and the palm sugar has completely dissolved. Whisk in the coconut milk and simmer vigorously for 7–10 minutes until thick and glossy, then remove from the heat and whisk in the vanilla extract and salt. Transfer to a suitable container and refrigerate until needed.

3. Place the apple halves flat-side down on a work surface and use a sharp knife to make thin cuts (do not cut the apples all the way through).

4. Place the apples flat-side down in the prepared dish and dust with the nutmeg and cinnamon. Melt the coconut oil and maple syrup together in a small saucepan before brushing over the apples, then loosely cover with foil and bake for 20 minutes until cooked through.

5. Remove the apples from the oven and carefully transfer to individual serving dishes or a large sharing platter. Drizzle over the caramel sauce and scatter over the crushed walnuts before serving.

'DOLE WHIP' NICE CREAM

SERVES 4

Unless you're a die-hard Disney fan like me you're probably wondering what on earth 'Dole whip' is. Let me tell you, you are in for a treat. On a baking hot day, having traipsed through just about every land the Magic Kingdom has to offer, you will find yourself at a stall selling what I can only describe as heaven in a plastic cup. If you like soft-serve ice cream and have a penchant for pineapple then this, my friends, is exactly what you've been waiting for. Made using fresh pineapple, unlike the Disney version (although that too is 100 per cent vegan!), this dairy-free delight is precisely what the doctor ordered, whether you're sweating it out in Florida or sitting in your backyard in Blighty. Bliss, I tell you. Bliss.

**1 small pineapple, peeled and cut into rough
chunks
2 ripe bananas, peeled and cut into rough
chunks
grated zest and juice of 1 lime
3 tablespoons maple syrup or agave nectar**

1.   Put the pineapple and banana chunks into zip-lock bags, transfer to the freezer and freeze overnight.

2.   The next day, place the frozen pineapple and banana chunks in a food processor along with the rest of the ingredients. Pulse to break the ingredients down before blending for 2–3 minutes, stopping and scraping down the sides from time to time, until the mixture resembles soft-whip ice cream (it will go through several stages to get to this point, so be patient). Spoon into tall glasses and serve immediately.

MATCHA & LIME PIE

with macerated strawberries

SERVES 8–10

The vibrant green hue of this (nearly) no-bake dessert coupled with the insane red of the macerated strawberries is precisely why I love to wheel this dish out at dinner parties – after all, we do eat with our eyes. The agar agar flakes ensure a firm pie that slices beautifully. If you are unfamiliar with this handy little ingredient, you'll soon get the hang of using it. The trick is to allow the flakes to dissolve in water without stirring (although occasional swirling is encouraged) before pouring the liquid into the cashew/tofu mix. You'll end up with a wonderfully zesty filling with an uplifting hint of matcha, which helpfully boosts both flavour and colour too – double whammy. Your friends and family are bound to be impressed.

Crust

100g desiccated coconut
100g pistachios
100g Brazil nuts
200g dried apricots
¼ teaspoon vanilla powder or ½ vanilla pod, split and seeds scraped
pinch of sea salt flakes
1 tablespoon coconut oil

Filling

200g cashew nuts, soaked overnight and drained (see page 8)

150g silken tofu
grated zest and juice of 6 limes
125ml agave nectar or maple syrup
1 heaped tablespoon matcha powder
pinch of sea salt flakes
250ml water
2 tablespoons agar agar flakes

Macerated strawberries

200g strawberries, hulled and sliced
juice of 1 lime
½ vanilla pod, seeds scraped
3 tablespoons palm sugar

1. Preheat the oven to 200°C (180°C fan), Gas Mark 6

2. To make the crust, place the desiccated coconut, pistachios and Brazil nuts in a blender or food processor and pulse together to form a fine crumb-like texture. Add the apricots, vanilla powder, salt and coconut oil and blend for 1 minute, or until it just comes together (pinch some of the mixture between your fingers to test – if it sticks easily, you're good to go).

3. Transfer the crust mixture to a 23cm fluted tart tin and press into the base and sides to cover evenly. Bake for 8–10 minutes, or until lightly coloured, then remove from the oven and leave to cool in the refrigerator until needed.

4. For the filling, add the cashew nuts to a blender together with the tofu, lime zest and juice, agave nectar, matcha powder and salt. Blend for 10–15 minutes, or until the mixture is completely smooth. (If it is not entirely silky, keep blending until you achieve the desired consistency, otherwise it will negatively affect the texture.)

5. Meanwhile, place the water in a small saucepan and sprinkle over the agar agar. Do not stir. Bring to the boil, then simmer over a medium heat for 5–10 minutes, or until the agar agar has dissolved and the water has reduced by about a third.

6. Add the agar agar liquid to the blender with the pie filling and blend until it is completely incorporated, scraping down the sides from time to time, then pour the filling over the cooled crust, smoothing the top with the back of a spatula. Cover with clingfilm and refrigerate for 4–6 hours, or until set.

7. For the macerated strawberries, put the berries, lime juice, vanilla seeds and palm sugar into a bowl, stir to combine and refrigerate for at least 30 minutes, or until needed, bringing the berries to room temperature before serving.

8. Pile the strawberries over the centre of the pie to serve.

WATERMELON WEDGE PARTY CAKE

SERVES 8-10

Party food doesn't necessarily have to be unhealthy. While sugar-laden cakes are a welcome occasional treat, sometimes I like to serve something that is both equal amounts virtuous and yummy. There is no conceivable way your guests will be disappointed with this quirky little fruit cake, especially once you cut into it and reveal its uber-pink interior – cue the 'wows'. The toasted coconut gives it some wonderful crunch, while the lightly whipped coconut cream exudes 'excuse me while I lick the bowl' factor in abundance. A terrific option for a kids' party (especially if they've already loaded up on sweeties and whatnot), this cake is an easy way to bring things down a notch in the chaos department without them feeling like they're being cheated. Win-win.

1 small seedless watermelon
250ml carton coconut cream, chilled
grated zest and juice of ½ lime
3 tablespoons agave nectar
50g toasted coconut flakes
4–5 strawberries, halved, to decorate

1. Slice both ends off the watermelon and place it cut-end down on a chopping board. Using a sharp knife cut away the remaining rind to create a loose cake-like shape, trimming the sides to square things up a little. Transfer to a serving plate.

2. Place the chilled coconut cream in a stand mixer, add the lime zest and juice and agave nectar and beat on a high speed until thick, fluffy and cloud-like (alternatively, put everything in a bowl and beat together use a hand-held electric whisk). Refrigerate for 10 minutes to chill and firm.

3. Once chilled, dollop the whipped coconut cream on top of the watermelon and ease it down the sides with a spatula to coat – don't worry if it slides off to begin with, just work it up the sides until it adheres. Scatter over the toasted coconut and decorate with fresh strawberries. Time to party!

COCONUT & CARDAMOM MACAROONS

with a simple chocolate coating

MAKES 12 MACAROONS

These easy macaroons were created with my mum in mind. Since going plant-based, they are the one treat she really misses, as unfortunately most shop-bought varieties contain egg. The cardamom is a classic inclusion, which is complemented by the touch of lemon (although lime would also be lovely). But what's particularly great about these macaroons is that they can be either baked or chilled to equally yummy effect. Quite honestly I can't decide which version I prefer. Dipped and drizzled in chocolate – the darker the better – they've fast become one of my favourite sweet treats, and thankfully my mum likes them too. You can shape the mixture into small bars, rather than mounds, if you prefer.

8 cardamom pods
200g desiccated coconut
grated zest of 1 lemon
125ml agave nectar or other vegan sweetener
1 vanilla pod, split lengthways and seeds
    scraped
3 tablespoons coconut cream
1 heaped tablespoon coconut oil
50g crushed pistachios

Coating
2 tablespoons coconut oil
3 tablespoons raw cacao powder
1 tablespoon rose water
2 tablespoons agave or maple syrup
pinch of pink Himalayan salt

1. If baking the macaroons, preheat the oven to 200°C (180°C fan), Gas Mark 6 and line a baking tray with baking paper.

2. Remove the seeds from the cardamom pods and grind to a fine powder in a pestle and mortar.

3. Place the ground cardamom in a food processor along with the desiccated coconut, coconut cream, lemon zest, agave nectar, vanilla seeds and coconut oil. Pulse until the mixture comes together. To test, pinch a small amount between your fingers – if it adheres easily it's ready to shape.

4. Take a tablespoon of the coconut mixture, shape it into a mound and place it on the prepared baking tray. Repeat with the rest of the mixture, then bake the macaroons for 10–12 minutes until golden before setting aside to cool, or simply refrigerate them for 30 minutes until firm.

5. To make the coating, melt the coconut oil in a small saucepan over a low–medium heat. Remove from the heat and add the cacao powder, rose water, agave syrup and salt. Gently stir until the mixture thickens and becomes smooth and glossy. If the mixture appears grainy, return the pan to a low heat and stir for a few seconds until the texture changes.

6. Dip the bottom of each macaroon in the cacao mixture to coat, then transfer to a baking sheet. Once all the macaroons have been dipped, drizzle the remaining coating over the tops and sprinkle over the pistachios. Let the chocolate coating set slightly, then return to the refrigerator for 30 minutes, or until the chocolate coating has hardened completely. Enjoy straightaway or keep in an airtight container in the refrigerator for up to 1 week.

DAIRY-FREE HAZELNUT & CHOCOLATE SPREAD

MAKES APPROX. 150G

Nut butters are easier to make than you'd imagine – all it takes is a little patience with the food processor. This spread is as wonderful on toast as it is dolloped in porridge or even straight from the jar.

150g hazelnuts

1 heaped tablespoon raw cacao powder

3 tablespoons maple syrup

100ml almond or soy milk

¼ teaspoon ground cinnamon

pinch of sea salt flakes

1. Preheat the oven to 220°C (200°C fan), Gas Mark 7.

2. Place the hazelnuts on a baking tray, transfer to the oven and toast for 5–7 minutes, shaking the pan from time to time, until lightly golden.

3. Remove the nuts from the oven and leave to cool before placing them in a clean tea towel and rubbing them vigorously to remove the skins. Transfer to a food processor and pulse to form a rough crumb-like consistency.

4. Add the cacao, maple syrup, plant milk, cinnamon and salt to the processor and blend together until the mixture forms a smooth, spreadable paste – loosening the mixture with a little extra plant milk if necessary. Transfer to a clean jar and keep refrigerated for up to 14 days.

BRAZIL-NUT CHAI STEAMER

SERVES 2

When I was at drama school in London, we would often have a morale-saving 'steamer' at the coffee shop in King's Cross Station. This is my homage to those ice-cold days, being told we'd never make it…

5 cardamom pods

100g Brazil nuts

½ cinnamon stick

¼ teaspoon vanilla powder

3 tablespoons agave nectar

¼ teaspoon black pepper

pinch of sea salt flakes

1 star anise

5–6 cloves

¼ teaspoon ground cinnamon, to serve

1. Remove the cardamom seeds from their pods and grind to a fine powder with a pestle and mortar.

2. Place the ground cardamom, Brazil nuts, cinnamon stick, vanilla powder, agave nectar, black pepper, salt and 600ml filtered water in a blender and blend until smooth.

3. Strain the mixture through a nut milk bag, muslin cloth or sieve, then transfer the milk to a saucepan and add the star anise and cloves. Heat gently over a very low heat, stirring continuously, until the mixture is steaming – being sure not to let it boil or simmer.

4. Pour into warmed cups or glasses and dust with a little cinnamon before serving.

SWEETLY DOES IT

CHOCOLATE CHIA OATMEAL COOKIES

MAKES 6 LARGE COOKIES

On the face of it, this recipe really shouldn't work. It makes a wet, sticky batter that doesn't hold a lot of promise. And yet, once it's baked, you're left with a soft, moreish cookie that is perfect with a cold glass of almond milk (my preference) and happens to be pretty darn good for you too – hurrah! Refined sugar-free and packed full of so-called superfoods (chia, cacao, cinnamon and the rest), these cookies will soon become a go-to recipe in your kitchen too. Personally, I prefer to make them in small batches, otherwise the temptation to consume them all in one sitting is too great, but you could easily double the quantities if you're expecting a crowd. I think they make a particularly good addition to any girls' night in – just add prosecco and it's a party!

100g spelt flour
50g rolled oats
1 tablespoon chia seeds
½ teaspoon baking powder
¼ teaspoon sea salt flakes, plus extra
    to decorate
½ teaspoon ground cinnamon, plus extra
    to decorate
1 tablespoon raw cacao powder or cocoa
2 tablespoons agave nectar
2 tablespoons maple syrup

1 tablespoon black treacle
50g coconut oil, melted
1 tablespoon plant milk (*see* page 9) or water
30g dried cranberries and/or plain dark
    chocolate chips

Coating
100g good-quality plain dark chocolate
    (70% cocoa solids), broken into pieces
1 tablespoon agave nectar
pinch of sea salt flakes

1. Preheat the oven to 200°C (180°C fan), Gas Mark 6 and line a baking tray with baking paper.
2. In a large bowl, whisk together the flour, oats, chia seeds, baking powder, salt, cinnamon and cacao until combined.
3. Add the agave nectar, maple syrup and black treacle to a small bowl and stir to combine. Make a well in the centre of the flour, pour over the coconut oil, agave and maple mixture and plant milk and gently fold to form a wet, sticky dough.
4. Stir the cranberries and chocolate chips through the dough, then dollop a heaped tablespoon on to the prepared sheet and shape it using 2 spoons. Repeat until all the mixture is used, leaving roughly 5cm between the cookies to allow for spreading.
5. Bake for 10–12 minutes until lightly golden but still nice and soft, then remove from the oven, transfer to a wire rack and leave to cool.
6. For the coating, place the chocolate, agave nectar and salt in a bowl set over a saucepan of lightly simmering water and melt gently, stirring, until completely smooth.
7. Drizzle the melted chocolate mixture over the cooled cookies and finish with a pinch of sea salt and a dusting of cinnamon. Enjoy with almond milk – or prosecco!

CHOCOLATE ORANGE POTS

with a toasted hazelnut & cacao nib crumb

SERVES 4

More like a pudding than a mousse, this rich dessert is only sinful in its sheer simplicity. Silken tofu really comes into its own here and the intense citrus flavour brings back fond memories of Terry's Chocolate Orange (those sickly sweet segments were such a treat) though it also works well with coffee extract. I can't tell you how many times this easy treat has saved me on the dinner party front; and while the mixture benefits from being chilled, I have frequently served it straight from the blender, dolloped into teeny tumblers and garnished with the toasted hazelnut and cacao nib crumb. I haven't received any complaints yet.

350g silken tofu
100g good-quality plain dark chocolate
    (70% cocoa solids), broken into pieces
2 tablespoons agave nectar (or 3 tablespoons
    maple syrup)
1 teaspoon orange extract
pinch of sea salt flakes

orange rind strips, to decorate

Toasted hazelnut and cacao nib crumb
50g toasted hazelnuts
1 tablespoon cacao nibs
pinch of sea salt flakes

1. Add the tofu to a food processor and blend until smooth.
2. Place the chocolate in a bowl set over a saucepan of lightly simmering water and melt gently, stirring, until completely smooth.
3. Remove the bowl from the heat and leave the chocolate for 5 minutes to cool slightly, then transfer to the food processor along with the agave nectar, orange extract and salt. Blend for 5–7 minutes until smooth, scraping down the sides with a spatula from time to time.
4. Pour the mixture into 4 ramekins or small glasses. Refrigerate for 2–3 hours.
5. To make the crumb, place the toasted hazelnuts, cacao nibs and salt in a small blender or food processor and pulse together to form a coarse crumb-like texture.
6. Sprinkle the crumb over the pots and decorate with a few strips of orange rind just before serving.

MULLED POACHED PEARS

with a silky lemon & thyme cashew cream

SERVES 6

A fabulously easy festive dessert, this exquisite mulled pear dish is truly a thing of beauty. Even if you're not much of a wine drinker, these are worth sampling for their soft-spiced sweetness alone. Served with the delicately infused lemon cashew cream, these pears add a touch of elegance to any gathering – just be sure to blend the cashew cream until silky smooth as there shouldn't be any hint of it having once been a nut. I tend to make both elements in advance, making this recipe a terrific option for a stress-free evening that can be spent socializing rather than sweating in the kitchen. Perfect.

750ml red wine
60ml sloe gin (optional, but lovely)
175g brown sugar
1 cinnamon stick
2 star anise
1 tablespoon cloves
1 bay leaf
rind of ½ orange
3 large pears (any variety), peeled and cut in
  half lengthways with the stalk intact

Lemon & thyme cashew cream
200g cashew nuts
1 thyme sprig, plus extra leaves to decorate
100ml water, plus extra if necessary
grated zest and juice of 1 lemon
1 teaspoon lemon extract
1 heaped tablespoon coconut oil
50ml agave nectar
pinch of fine sea salt flakes

1. For the lemon and thyme cream, place the cashew nuts and thyme in a large bowl and cover with freshly boiled water. Set aside to soak and infuse for at least 6 hours, preferably overnight.

2. Drain and rinse the cashew nuts and place in a blender along with the remaining ingredients. Blend for at least 10 minutes until completely smooth, scraping down the sides periodically with a spatula and adding an extra splash of water if necessary. Transfer to a bowl and refrigerate until needed.

3. Place the wine, gin (if using), sugar, cinnamon, star anise, cloves, bay leaf and orange rind in a large saucepan and bring to the boil, then reduce the heat to a gentle simmer.

4. Gently lower the pear halves into the pan and simmer for 20 minutes, or until soft, inserting a toothpick into the flesh to test. Turn the heat off and leave the pears to sit in the warm liquid for a further 10 minutes, then carefully remove the pears from the pan and set aside.

5. Bring the poaching liquid to the boil and cook for 10–15 minutes, or until reduced to a thick, pourable syrup.

6. To serve, place a dollop or two of cashew cream on the bottom of each dish, top each with a pear half and drizzle over the reduced mulled wine syrup. Scatter over a few extra thyme leaves to finish.

CACAO NIB GRANOLA CLUSTERS

MAKES 6–8 SERVINGS

If you're as obsessed with granola as I am then you'll likely be into this recipe. The ultimate in both cluster and crunch, this granola has the ability to bridge three eating opportunities in one fell swoop – breakfast, dessert and mid-morning/afternoon/early-evening snack. OK, that's clearly more than three, but when something tastes this good, who's counting? With me and my husband regularly reaching into the granola jar, it's sometimes lucky to last a day, but should it make it past the 24-hour mark, I tumble it into my breakfast yogurt or smoothie bowl or use it as a topping for ice cream. The granola might seem spongy when you first remove it from the oven so be sure to let it cool completely before consuming for the full crunch effect.

100g rolled oats
100g desiccated coconut
50g cacao nibs
1 heaped tablespoon raw cacao powder or
   cocoa
1 teaspoon ground cinnamon (optional)
8–10 medjool dates, pitted
4 dried figs

30g dried cherries or raisins
pinch of sea salt flakes

To serve
dairy-free yogurt, homemade plant milk
   (*see* page 9) or 'Dole Whip' Nice Cream
   (*see* page 190)

1. Preheat the oven to 170°C (150°C fan), Gas Mark 3½. Line a large baking sheet with baking paper.
2. Place the oats, coconut and cacao nibs in a food processor and pulse to break up the pieces, then sprinkle over the cacao powder and cinnamon and pulse to combine. Add the dates, figs, cherries and salt and blend together for 2–3 minutes until the mixture forms sticky clumps.
3. Tip the mixture out on to the prepared baking sheet and spread it out so it forms a uniform layer. Transfer to the oven and bake for 15 minutes, then gently turn the clusters using a spatula. Bake for a further 10 minutes until the clusters begin to harden and firm.
4. Remove from the oven and leave the granola to cool completely before transferring to a jar. Serve with dairy-free yogurt, homemade plant milk or 'Dole whip' nice cream.

SCHOOL CANTEEN
'TRIPLE MINT CHOC' BISCUIT SLICE

MAKES 8

This biscuit slice conjures up memories of break time, with hordes of schoolgirls streaming towards the canteen in a bid to snaffle any homemade delights that might be on offer. I always made a beeline for the mint chocolate slice, which has lingered on my mind (and taste buds) ever since. Slightly healthier than the original but no less moreish, this is still something of treat and so I reserve it for when friends come over for coffee. It's a perennial gluten-free winner. I'm convinced my younger self would approve.

Base
100g Brazil nuts
50g cacao nibs
4 medjool dates, pitted
pinch of sea salt flakes

Filling
1 tablespoon coconut oil
100g good-quality dark chocolate, chopped
(70% cocoa solids)
2 tablespoons tahini

½ tablespoon agave nectar
1 teaspoon peppermint extract
pinch of sea salt flakes

Topping
2 tablespoons coconut oil, plus extra
if necessary
3 tablespoons raw cacao powder or cocoa
1 tablespoon agave nectar
pinch of sea salt flakes

1. Line a 900g loaf tin with baking paper.
2. To make the base, place the Brazil nuts and cacao nibs in a food processor and blitz to a rough breadcrumb-like consistency. Add the medjool dates and salt, and blitz again until the mixture comes together and is reasonably sticky to the touch.
3. Spread the mixture over the base of the tin, pushing it into the edges and pressing it down in an even layer. Transfer to the refrigerator and leave to chill for around 30 minutes, or until reasonably firm.
4. For the filling, heat the coconut oil in a saucepan over a low heat. Add the chocolate to the pan and swirl gently until completely melted, then remove from the heat, add the tahini, agave nectar, peppermint extract and salt and whisk together vigorously until smooth and glossy. Pour the filling into the loaf tin over the chilled base, spreading the mixture to the edges with a spatula, and refrigerate for at least 1 hour, or until set.
5. To make the topping, melt the coconut oil in another saucepan over a low–medium heat. Add the cacao powder, agave and salt and gently stir together until smooth and glossy – if the mixture is looking a little grainy, simply add an extra small knob of coconut oil to loosen it. Pour the topping over the set filling and tip the tin from side to side until it reaches the edges, then return the tin to the refrigerator and leave to chill for several hours, or ideally overnight.
6. To serve, remove the slice from the refrigerator, using the paper to lift it from the tin, and cut it into small squares. Eat straightaway, or keep in an airtight container in the refrigerator for up to 1 week.

PANNA COTTA THREE WAYS

SERVES 2–4

I'm fairly fussy when it comes to dessert. Because I don't indulge in it that often, when I do it has to be a little bit special. These easy panna cottas are just that. You could say that this is simply jelly for grown-ups, but that shouldn't mean they don't invite some excitement when brought to the table. Perhaps it's their funny wibble (technical term) or maybe it's the ceaseless versatility on the flavour front, but I just can't seem to get enough of them. It also helps that they can be made well in advance, which saves any stress when you have guests. These are my current top three varieties – I love their subtle sweetness and soothing beige hues – but feel free to experiment here yourself. I can't wait to see what you come up with.

1.

VANILLA PANNA COTTA

250ml water
2 heaped teaspoons agar agar flakes
1 vanilla pod
4 tablespoons caster sugar
250ml soy cream
1 teaspoon vanilla extract

Blueberry compote
150g blueberries
juice of ½ lemon
3 tablespoons sugar

1. Place the water in a small saucepan and sprinkle over the agar agar. Do not stir. Bring to the boil, then simmer over a medium heat for 5–10 minutes until the agar agar has dissolved.

2. Split the vanilla pod lengthways and scrape the seeds into the pan. Add the pod to the pan with the sugar and simmer for a further 3–5 minutes, or until the sugar has dissolved.

3. Whisk in the soy cream and cook gently for 1–2 minutes, then take the saucepan off the heat and whisk in the vanilla extract. Set aside and allow to cool slightly.

4. Pour the mixture into 2 large moulds or 4 small glasses. Refrigerate for at least 6 hours, or ideally overnight.

5. To make the compote, place the blueberries in a small saucepan with the lemon juice and sugar. Bring to a gentle simmer and cook for 10–15 minutes until the blueberries release their juices and begin to soften. Take off the heat, leave to cool and refrigerate until ready to serve.

6. Remove the panna cotta from the refrigerator 5 minutes prior to serving. Place a plate on top of the mould, carefully turn upside down and shake gently to release the jelly.

7. Serve with the blueberry compote.

2.

COFFEE PANNA COTTA WITH PINE NUT CREAM

250ml water
2 heaped teaspoons agar agar flakes
3 tablespoons light brown sugar
pinch of sea salt flakes
250ml carton coconut cream, chilled
1 x 30ml espresso coffee shot
20g shaved dark chocolate (70% cocoa
    solids), to decorate

Pine nut cream
100g pine nuts, soaked and drained
    (see page 8), plus 2–3 tablespoons of the
    soaking liquid
2–3 tablespoons maple syrup
pinch of sea salt flakes

1. To make the pine nut cream, place the pine nuts in a small blender along with the reserved soaking liquid, maple syrup and salt and blend until completely smooth and thick.

2. Place the water in a small saucepan and sprinkle over the agar agar. Do not stir. Bring to the boil, then simmer over a medium heat for 5–10 minutes until the agar agar has dissolved.

3. Whisk in the sugar and salt and simmer for a further 3–5 minutes, or until the sugar has dissolved.

4. Whisk in the coconut cream and espresso and cook gently for 2–3 minutes, then take the saucepan off the heat and allow to cool slightly.

5. Pour the mixture into 2 ramekins or 4 small glasses. Refrigerate for at least 6 hours, or ideally overnight.

6. Remove the panna cotta from the refrigerator 5 minutes prior to serving. Place a plate on top of the mould, carefully turn upside down and shake gently to release the jelly.

7. Sprinkle over the chocolate shavings to decorate and serve with the pine nut cream.

3.

CHAI PANNA COTTA

250ml water
2 heaped teaspoons agar agar flakes
4 tablespoons coconut palm sugar
1 small cinnamon stick
4 cardamom pods
6 cloves
1 star anise
good grinding of black pepper
pinch of sea salt flakes

¼ teaspoon vanilla powder or 1 teaspoon
  vanilla extract
250ml canned coconut milk
1 tablespoon toasted flaked almonds,
  to decorate

Whipped coconut cream
200ml canned coconut cream, chilled
1 tablespoon agave nectar

1. For the whipped coconut cream, place the coconut cream and agave nectar in a mixing bowl and whisk together until light and fluffy. Transfer to the refrigerator and leave for at least 20 minutes to chill and firm.

2. Meanwhile, place the water in a small saucepan and sprinkle over the agar agar. Do not stir. Bring to the boil, then simmer over a medium heat for 5–10 minutes until the agar agar has dissolved.

3. Whisk in the palm sugar, cinnamon stick, cardamom pods, cloves, star anise, black pepper, salt and vanilla powder and simmer for 3–5 minutes, or until the sugar has dissolved.

4. Stir in the coconut milk and cook gently for 2–3 minutes until smooth and silky, then take the saucepan off the heat and allow to cool slightly.

5. Pour the mixture into 2 ramekins or 4 small glasses. Refrigerate for at least 6 hours, or ideally overnight.

6. Remove the panna cotta from the refrigerator 5 minutes prior to serving. Place a plate on top of the mould, carefully turn upside down and shake gently to release the jelly.

7. Dollop a spoonful of coconut yogurt on top of each jelly, then sprinkle over the toasted flaked almonds and serve.

GRAPEFRUIT, GIN & SAGE GRANITA

SERVES 4–6

So refreshing and light, granita is the perfect palate cleanser – and when spiked with a decent dose of gin it becomes the perfect aperitif too. With zero skill required to create it (save the scraping, which isn't exactly hard), I find myself experimenting with granita's endless versatility on a semi-regular basis. Its soothing, melt-in-your-mouth qualities make it particularly desirable on a piercingly hot summer day. Serve this in chilled glasses and add another splash of gin just before serving for the ultimate adult slushie.

100g caster sugar
grated zest and juice of 1 grapefruit
10g sage, plus extra to decorate
250ml water
75ml gin, plus extra to serve

1. Add the sugar, grapefruit zest and juice, sage and measured water to a saucepan and bring to the boil. Reduce the heat to a simmer and cook for 1–2 minutes, or until the sugar has completely dissolved. Remove from the heat and set aside to cool.

2. Strain the cooled sugar syrup through a fine-mesh sieve and add it to a blender along with the gin. Pulse together briefly to combine, then pour into a suitable dish or container and freeze for 1 hour.

3. Remove the granita from the freezer and scrape with a fork to break up the ice crystals, then return to the freezer. Repeat the process every 30 minutes for 2–3 hours, or until you have achieved the desired consistency.

4. To serve, spoon the granita into small chilled tumblers or glasses and decorate each with a small sage leaf. Splash over a little extra gin and serve.

PISTACHIO & POMEGRANATE KULFI

SERVES 6–8

I have broken at least two ice cream machines in my time and so in lieu of having said equipment to hand, I've come to rely on the equally delicious Indian ice cream alternative – kulfi. Simmered and reduced until it has an almost condensed milk-like consistency, kulfi has a noticeably denser texture than other frozen desserts and is also very, very sweet. The pistachio paste upon which its magnificence is built is absolutely crucial to its success. For a purer, brighter colour, I recommend using skinned pistachios – you can lightly toast them in the oven to make the skins easier to rub off if you can't find them like this. A teaspoon of matcha also goes a long way to boost the colour without interfering with the overall flavour. I personally adore the nutty texture here but if you prefer a smoother finish, simply add a touch more water – an extra 100ml or so – at the blending stage and squeeze the mixture through a nut milk bag before reducing it on the hob.

100g skinned pistachios
300ml water
400ml canned coconut milk
175g raw cane sugar
½ small cinnamon stick
3–4 cardamom pods

pinch of pink Himalayan salt
½ tablespoon rosewater
70g pomegranate seeds, plus extra
    to decorate
handful of dried edible rose petals

1. Line a 450g loaf tin with clingfilm or baking paper.
2. Add the pistachios and measured water to a blender and blitz together for up to 10 minutes until smooth, scraping down the sides from time to time as you go. Transfer to a large pan along with the coconut milk, sugar, cinnamon stick and cardamom pods and salt, bring to a simmer and cook for 1 hour until thickened and reduced by at least a third.
3. Remove from the heat and leave to cool slightly before whisking in the rosewater. Set aside for 20–30 minutes, or until completely cool.
4. Stir the pomegranate seeds through the cooled mixture, pour it into the prepared loaf tin and freeze for at least 2 hours, or until set.
5. To remove from the mould, place the tin in a shallow bowl of freshly boiled water for a few seconds. Put a plate on top and carefully turn it over, then tap gently until the kulfi slips out. Remove the baking paper and let it thaw for 5 minutes before cutting into thick slices and adorning with dried rose petals and a few extra pomegranate seeds.

BAKING
BRILLIANCE

COFFEE CELEBRATION CAKE

SERVES 10–12

Being a coffee fanatic, I can't think of a better way to celebrate than to inject some caffeine into this fun three-tiered cake. With a perfectly nutty crumb, it finishes any grown-up gathering with a bang. Vegan baking is usually accompanied by an air of trepidation, but this simple recipe will put those fears to bed. The cake layers won't rise tremendously but once they're stacked and slathered in icing, everything will begin to make sense. This cake also happens to benefit from being made in advance, giving the flavours ample time to come to the fore – don't worry, it remains surprisingly moist and slices wonderfully too. Pop the kettle on, it's time for tea.

1 teaspoon balsamic vinegar
200ml soy milk
300g plain flour
1 tablespoon baking powder
1 teaspoon bicarbonate of soda
pinch of sea salt flakes
1 teaspoon vanilla powder or extract
   (optional)
100g vegetable shortening
100g dairy-free margarine
200g light brown sugar
60ml espresso coffee, cooled
1 tablespoon date or maple syrup
1 teaspoon coffee extract

Icing
150g vegetable shortening
150g dairy-free margarine
500g icing sugar, plus extra if necessary
1 teaspoon coffee extract

To decorate
75g shaved dark chocolate
   (70% cocoa solids)
75g toasted almonds

1. Preheat the oven to 200°C (180°C fan), Gas Mark 6. Line three 18cm shallow sponge tins with baking paper.

2. Combine the balsamic vinegar and soy milk in a bowl and set aside for 5–10 minutes to let the mixture curdle.

3. Place the flour, baking powder, bicarbonate of soda, salt and vanilla powder, if using, in a mixing bowl and whisk gently to combine.

4. Beat the shortening, margarine and sugar together in a separate bowl until light and fluffy.

5. Whisk the curdled soy mixture, espresso, date syrup and coffee extract together until combined, then pour half over the creamed butter and sugar mixture. Add two-thirds of the flour and gently fold to combine, then fold in the remaining liquid and flour mixtures to form a batter.

6. Divide the batter evenly between the prepared cake tins and bake for 25 minutes, or until a cake tester or skewer inserted into the centre comes out clean. Set the sponges aside for at least 5 minutes to cool slightly before gently removing from the tin, then transfer to a wire rack and leave to cool completely.

7. Using an electric whisk or stand mixer, beat the icing ingredients together until light and fluffy,

adding a little more icing sugar if necessary to ensure the icing holds its shape. Refrigerate until needed.

8. To assemble the cake, dot a cake stand with a little icing, then lay the first sponge down and press gently to secure. Spread the first layer with the icing before placing another sponge on top, then repeat until all the layers are sandwiched together. Carefully spread the remaining icing over the cake, easing it down the sides and smoothing it with a spatula to coat evenly.

9. Decorate the sides of the cake with shaved chocolate and scatter toasted almonds over the top before serving.

ALL-OUT CHOCOLATE HONEYCOMB LOAF

SERVES 8-10

This recipe has a special place in my heart because I made a version of it for my dad's 70th birthday. He had been following a fairly strict plant-based diet (with very little sugar) but for his party he wanted something a little bit special, and I duly delivered. The honeycomb shards make an incredible visual impact and I guarantee people will be practically fighting over who gets to eat the last one. This all-out loaf is a terrifically easy recipe to add to your vegan-baking repertoire.

120g plain flour	**Honeycomb**
70g granulated sugar	200g caster sugar
30g raw cacao powder or cocoa	4 tablespoons golden syrup
1 teaspoon baking powder	1½ teaspoons bicarbonate of soda
½ teaspoon bicarbonate of soda	
1 banana	**Icing**
3 tablespoons olive oil	3 tablespoons dairy-free margarine
120ml plant milk (*see page 9*)	100g icing sugar
1 teaspoon vanilla extract	1 heaped tablespoon raw cacao powder or cocoa

1.   Preheat the oven to 190°C (170°C fan), Gas Mark 5. Lightly oil a 450g loaf tin and line a large baking tray with baking paper.

2.   Whisk the flour, sugar, cocoa, baking powder and bicarbonate of soda together in a large bowl.

3.   Mash the banana and whisk together with the oil, plant milk and vanilla extract until smooth.

4.   Make a well in the centre of the flour mixture, spoon over the wet ingredients and gently fold together to form a batter.

5.   Spoon the batter into the prepared tin, tapping it firmly on your worktop to get rid of any air bubbles. Bake for 30–35 minutes, or until lightly golden on top and a cake tester or skewer inserted into the centre comes out clean. Remove from the oven and leave in the tin for at least 5 minutes to cool slightly, then transfer to a wire rack and leave to cool completely.

6.   Meanwhile, make the honeycomb. Mix the sugar and syrup together in a heavy-based saucepan set over a medium–high heat until combined and cook for 2–3 minutes until it begins to bubble. Simmer for a further 3–5 minutes, being sure not to stir as you go, until golden and smooth, then remove from the heat and quickly whisk in the bicarbonate of soda vigorously until the mixture bubbles before carefully turning it out on to the lined baking tray. Leave to cool completely before breaking into shards.

7.   For the icing, beat everything together with an electric whisk or stand mixer until smooth. Refrigerate until needed.

8.   When ready to eat, spread the chocolate icing over the top and sides of the loaf evenly using a spatula and adorn it with the shards of honeycomb. Serve.

BLUEBERRY UPSIDE-DOWN CAKE

with a macadamia cream icing

SERVES 8–10

Nuts are the cornerstone of my cooking, and their versatility never ceases to amaze me. Here, I've blended them to a flour to give this polenta cake a little more girth. You could use shop-bought ground almonds or pistachio nuts, but I think the slightly nubbly texture of home-blitzed nuts really adds to the overall result. Polenta cakes are often a fine balance of polenta (unsurprisingly) and whatever else you choose to pair it with – plain flour works well, but because I wanted to make this a gluten-free affair, I went with a mixture of nuts and gram flour. This way the cake can get by without an official binder (such as flaxseeds or chia) as the small amount of gram flour added ensures that it holds together beautifully and possesses a rather wonderful crumb. Plant-based baking at its natural best.

100g almonds	Macadamia cream
50g pistachios	100g macadamias, soaked and drained
75g polenta	(*see* page 8)
25g gram (chickpea) flour	75ml reserved pineapple juice
1½ teaspoons baking powder	½ teaspoon lemon extract
pinch of sea salt flakes	2 tablespoons agave nectar
100g canned pineapple chunks, reserving	1 tablespoon maple syrup
the juice (see Macadamia cream)	pinch of sea salt flakes
juice of 1 lemon and zest of 2	
3 tablespoons soy yogurt	
125ml maple syrup	
75ml olive oil	
300g fresh blueberries	
2 tablespoons palm sugar	

1. Preheat the oven to 190°C (170°C fan), Gas Mark 5. Line a 20cm cake tin with baking paper.
2. Place the almonds and pistachios in a food processor and blitz to a fine flour. Transfer to a large mixing bowl and add the polenta, gram flour, baking powder, lemon zest and salt. Whisk to combine.
3. Place the pineapple chunks and lemon juice in a food processor and blitz to a rough purée. Transfer to a mixing bowl and whisk together with the soy yogurt and 100ml of the maple syrup to combine.
4. Make a well in the centre of the flour mixture, pour over the oil and the pineapple mixture and gently fold to form a batter.
5. Cover the bottom of the prepared cake tin with half the blueberries, then pour over the batter and bake for 1¼ hours, or until a cake tester or skewer inserted into the centre comes out clean. Remove from the oven and leave to cool for at least 5 minutes, before removing it from the tin (it's best to turn it upside down for a little while and leave it to rest for a while before trying this). Transfer to a wire rack and leave to cool completely.

6. Meanwhile, place the palm sugar in a saucepan along with the remaining blueberries and maple syrup. Bring to a simmer and cook over a medium heat for 5–10 minutes, or until syrupy. Set aside to cool.

7. To make the macadamia cream, add the macadamias to a food processor and blend to a rough paste before adding the pineapple juice, lemon extract, agave nectar, maple syrup and salt. Blend for up to 5 minutes until smooth and fluffy.

8. Once the cake has completely cooled, spoon the macadamia cream over the top and smooth it slightly so it almost meets the edges, then drizzle over the cooled blueberry syrup to finish.

ORANGE BLOSSOM & POPPY SEED SCONE BREAD

SERVES 4

As an Irishwoman, I have sampled my fair share of scone bread – usually in loaf form and almost always made with buttermilk. This version is unapologetically inauthentic, influenced by all three countries in which I have lived – namely England, Ireland and the United States. A hybrid of sorts, it hopefully takes the best of each nation and combines them to create a light, fluffy bread that can be broken into four sections, slathered in whatever you fancy (I heartily recommend marmalade) and served alongside a cup of tea. The subtle note of orange blossom elevates what is an embarrassingly easy recipe into something really quite elegant. I'm not sure my grandmother would approve, mind, but fortunately everyone I have served it to has loved it.

1 teaspoon cider vinegar

50ml soy milk

3 tablespoons agave nectar

grated zest and juice of ½ orange

½ tablespoon orange blossom water

175g plain flour

1 teaspoon baking powder

½ teaspoon bicarbonate of soda

1 tablespoon poppy seeds

pinch of sea salt flakes

50g dairy-free margarine, refrigerator-cold and cut into cubes

1. Preheat the oven to 220°C (200°C fan), Gas Mark 7.

2. Combine the cider vinegar and soy milk in a bowl and set aside for 5–10 minutes to let the mixture curdle.

3. Lightly whisk the soy milk mixture, agave nectar, orange juice and orange blossom water together in a bowl.

4. Place the flour, baking powder, bicarbonate of soda, orange zest, poppy seeds and salt in a large mixing bowl and mix to combine. Add the margarine to the bowl and work it into the flour with your fingertips until the mixture resembles breadcrumbs.

5. Make a well in the centre of the flour mixture, pour over the wet ingredients and gently fold together to form a dough.

6. Tip the dough on to a floured baking tray and shape it into a round using your hands, then cut it into quarters with a floured knife but don't separate (the pieces will pull apart easily when baked).

7. Bake for 12–15 minutes until risen and lightly golden, then remove from the oven and leave to cool completely before breaking into pieces and serving.

PLUM & ALMOND CAKE

with an Earl Grey pine nut cream

SERVES 6–8

Ground almonds (or 'almond flour' if we want to be fancy) are hands-down my favourite thing to use in vegan baking because they lend a cake moistness and density while still retaining an enviable crumb. Genius. As they act almost like a binder, I find I need very little else to ensure my cake turns out, well, 'cakey'. Of course, this recipe still contains sugar and margarine, so it's pretty far from being a health food, which is precisely why I like it. There's something so comforting about all that creaming, stirring, folding and waiting; it's easy to see why baking is like therapy to some, as you can't hurry it – or wing it, for that matter. Though the reward for me will always be in the eating, and in that respect this plum and almond affair is just the ticket.

1 teaspoon cider vinegar
80ml soy (or other plant) milk
100g dairy-free margarine
150g caster sugar
175g plain or white spelt flour
50g ground almonds
1½ teaspoons baking powder
½ teaspoon bicarbonate of soda
pinch of sea salt flakes
1 teaspoon almond extract

3 plums, cut into segments
2 tablespoons maple syrup

Earl Grey pine nut cream
100g pine nuts
200ml freshly brewed Earl Grey tea
1 tablespoon maple syrup
pinch of sea salt flakes
2–3 tablespoons water

1. To make the pine nut cream, place the pine nuts in a bowl and cover with the freshly brewed Earl Grey tea. Set aside to soak for 6 hours, or ideally overnight.

2. Preheat the oven to 210°C (190°C fan), Gas Mark 6½. Grease and line a 20cm cake tin.

3. Combine the cider vinegar and soy milk in a bowl and set aside for 5–10 minutes to let the mixture curdle.

4. Beat the margarine and sugar together until combined. Gradually sift in the flour, ground almonds, baking powder, bicarbonate of soda and salt and whisk together.

5. Add the almond extract to the soy milk and pour into the cake mixture. Fold to form a batter.

6. Pour into the prepared cake tin. Press the plum segments into the batter in concentric circles, overlapping a little if you like. Bake for 60 minutes, covering the top of the cake with baking paper for the final 15 minutes, or until a cake tester or skewer inserted into the centre of the cake comes out clean.

7. Meanwhile, drain the pine nuts, reserving a tablespoon or so of the soaking liquid and place in a small blender along with the reserved liquid, maple syrup, salt and water. Blend until completely smooth and thick.

8. Remove the cake from the oven, transfer to a wire rack and brush over the maple syrup. Leave to cool, then remove from the tin. Slice and serve with a generous dollop of pine nut cream.

EASY WHEATEN LOAF

SERVES 4-6

In my family home there was always a wheaten loaf on the kitchen counter. Granted, it may not have been homemade but nevertheless it was still pretty damn delicious. If you go to Ireland now you'll probably still be offered a slice with just about everything you order – soup, salad, even your main course; it's a bit of a national obsession. This vegan version is bang on the money, despite the absence of buttermilk. Because this recipe is dairy-free I'm using a plant-based baking trick, which is to curdle soy milk with a touch of cider vinegar. You won't believe the difference this makes to the overall texture and flavour of the bread – so much so that my kitchen counter now boasts its very own weekly wheaten loaf. Got to keep those traditions going!

1 teaspoon cider vinegar
300ml soy milk
200g rye flour, plus extra for dusting
200g plain flour
1 teaspoon bicarbonate of soda

½ teaspoon pink Himalayan salt
1 tablespoon maple syrup
½ tablespoon black treacle
1 tablespoon olive oil
½ tablespoon rolled oats

1. Preheat the oven to 220°C (200°C fan), Gas Mark 7. Grease a 450g loaf tin and dust the sides with a little flour.

2. Combine the cider vinegar and soy milk in a bowl and set aside for 5–10 minutes to let the mixture curdle.

3. Place the flours, bicarbonate of soda and salt in a large bowl and whisk together to combine.

4. Whisk the maple syrup, black treacle and oil together. Make a well in the centre of the flour and pour in the oil mixture along with the soy milk mixture. Use a spatula or fork to work the flour into the liquid in a gradual clockwise motion until it forms a rough dough.

5. Transfer the dough to the tin, spreading the mixture to the sides using a spatula. Sprinkle over the oats and dust with a little rye flour, then bake for 30 minutes, or until the bottom of the loaf sounds hollow when tapped.

6. Remove from the oven, cover with a clean tea towel and leave the bread to rest in the tin for 10 minutes before transferring it to a wire rack. Wrap in a clean tea towel and leave to cool to room temperature, then cut into slices and serve.

VEGAN PAVLOVA

with poached rhubarb & vanilla yogurt

SERVES 6–8

Pavlova – the holy grail of vegan desserts if ever there was one. Who would have thought that chickpea liquid would be the answer to our prayers? A stand mixer or electric mixer is pretty crucial here, and I advise whisking until it's as firm as you can humanly get it before transferring it to the tray. It's also crucial that you allow the meringue to cool completely in the oven before removing it. I like to make it a day in advance to avoid any meringue-induced meltdowns, but if you're not serving it immediately, be sure to keep it in an airtight container. If you prefer to make slightly smaller meringues, reduce the cooking time by about 30 minutes. Of course, the topping possibilities are endless but the pale pink of the rhubarb paired with the cool soft white of the yogurt is absolute perfection in my opinion. Enjoy!

100ml chilled aquafaba (reserved chickpea liquid)

½ teaspoon cream of tartar

125g caster sugar

400ml coconut yogurt (*see* page 40)

1 vanilla pod, split lengthways and seeds scraped

400g rhubarb, cut diagonally into 6cm chunks

4 tablespoons raw cane sugar

1 strip of lemon rind

1 lemon thyme sprig

1. Preheat the oven to 120°C (100°C fan), Gas Mark ½. Line a large baking sheet with baking paper.
2. Place the aquafaba in a stand mixer with the whisk attachment added and whisk on a medium setting until it becomes thick and frothy. (Alternatively, a large mixing bowl and hand-held electric whisk will work equally well, although it may be a little more tasking on the arms.)
3. Add the cream of tartar and whisk on high setting for at least 10 minutes until thick peaks begin to form. Gradually add the caster sugar, one tablespoon at a time, until it is glossy and thick – this may take anywhere up to 30 minutes but it is crucial the mixture is as stiff as possible, so be patient.
4. Secure the baking paper on the sheet with a dot of meringue under each corner, then spoon over the meringue and shape it into a rough rectangle using a spatula, spreading it out to almost meet the edges of the tray. Transfer to the oven and cook for 3½ hours, then turn off the heat and leave to cool completely in the oven for at least 6 hours, ideally overnight. Transfer to an airtight container until needed.
5. Whisk the coconut yogurt and vanilla seeds (reserving the pod) together to combine. Refrigerate until needed.
6. Place the rhubarb in a saucepan along with the cane sugar, lemon rind, thyme and vanilla pod. Pour over just enough water to cover (200–250ml), bring to a very gentle simmer and cook for 10–12 minutes, or until the rhubarb is just cooked through. Leave it to cool in the syrup, then refrigerate for several hours, or until needed.
7. To assemble, place the pavlova on a large platter and layer over the coconut yogurt first followed by the chilled rhubarb. Serve immediately and let everyone help themselves.

MINCEMEAT PINWHEELS

MAKES 18

Hands up who loves a cheat recipe! Truthfully, I often cringe at recipes like these but then I find myself turning to them time and again. Ready-made puff pastry is a year-round staple in my kitchen, a godsend for when unexpected guests pop round. I can't tell you how many times I've made these over the years – usually at Christmas, but not always – and it's sometimes worrying how well they are received, the 'oohs' and 'ahhs' leaving me almost offended on behalf of my other recipes. I like to roll the pastry out a touch before spreading it with an even layer of mincemeat, as it helps it crisp up. Be sure also to secure the ends of the pinwheels as they can have a tendency to unravel…although thankfully that doesn't affect the taste.

1 sheet of vegan ready-made puff pastry, thawed if frozen
½ tablespoon melted coconut oil
1½ teaspoons ground cinnamon
400g vegan mincemeat

1 teaspoon water or plant milk (*see page 9*)
30g flaked almonds
zest of ½ orange
icing sugar, to serve

1. Preheat the oven to 220°C (200°C fan), Gas Mark 7. Line a baking sheet with baking paper.
2. Roll the pastry out on to a lightly floured surface and brush with the melted coconut oil. Dust the entire sheet with 1 teaspoon of the ground cinnamon and spread the mincemeat over evenly, easing it to the edges using a spatula.
3. Starting from one of the short sides, roll the pastry up tightly into a log. Brush the ends with a little water or plant milk and secure firmly to ensure it doesn't unravel in the oven.
4. Cut the pastry log into 1cm pieces and place on a prepared baking sheet. Sprinkle over the flaked almonds, dust with the remaining ground cinnamon and bake for 15 minutes or until golden.
5. Transfer to a wire rack and leave to cool for at least 10 minutes. Scatter over the orange zest and dust generously with icing sugar to decorate before serving.

STICKY GINGERBREAD BITES

SERVES 10-12

I don't really play favourites when it comes to baking but I must say I have a serious weakness for gingerbread. More like a tray bake, these small squares are sticky sweet and seriously moist – perfect for eating alongside a festive cocktail. I like to pile them up high on a cake stand and either paint them with edible gold leaf or sprinkle them with gold dust. Demure they are not, and all the better for it.

110g plain flour
50g spelt flour
1 teaspoon baking powder
½ teaspoon bicarbonate of soda
1 teaspoon ground ginger
½ teaspoon ground cinnamon
½ teaspoon allspice
pinch of sea salt flakes
1 small banana
1 thumb-sized piece of fresh root ginger, peeled and grated
120g light brown sugar
1 tablespoon black treacle
1 tablespoon maple syrup
125ml soy milk (or other plant milk)

1 tablespoon water
1 tablespoon olive oil
½ tablespoon balsamic vinegar

Pomegranate glaze
3 tablespoons pomegranate juice
1 tablespoon satsuma juice
1 teaspoon pomegranate molasses
3 tablespoons agave nectar
1 tablespoon granulated sugar
1 tablespoon dairy-free margarine

To serve
handful of pomegranate seeds
edible gold leaf or dust (optional)

1. Preheat the oven to 190°C (170°C fan), Gas Mark 5. Line a 30 x 20cm brownie tin with baking paper.
2. Sift the flours, baking powder, bicarbonate of soda, spices and salt into a large bowl.
3. Mash the banana to a smooth purée and transfer to a separate bowl along with the grated ginger, sugar, black treacle, maple syrup, soy milk, water, oil and balsamic vinegar. Whisk thoroughly until completely combined.
4. Make a well in the centre of the flour, pour in the wet mixture and fold together gently to form a batter.
5. Pour the batter into the prepared tin and bake for 30 minutes until lightly golden. Remove from the oven and leave to cool slightly for 10 minutes before removing from the tin and transferring to a wire rack.
6. Meanwhile, add the glaze ingredients to a shallow frying pan. Bring to the boil, then reduce the heat to a simmer and cook for 10–15 minutes until reduced, thickened and syrupy.
7. While the bread is still warm, pour or brush over the glaze, covering it entirely. Sprinkle over a generous handful of pomegranate seeds and for a final, festive flourish, paint on some edible gold leaf or sprinkle over a little gold dust, if you fancy. Leave to cool completely before cutting into bite-sized squares.

CAKEY BAKED DOUGHNUTS

with a vibrant cashew icing

MAKES 6 DOUGHNUTS

These doughnuts are a cinch to make and taste just as good as the real thing. I rarely go in for foodie fads but my mini-doughnut tin gets so much use and I always have fun experimenting with icings and toppings. A glaze or drizzle works fine here – although they are good enough without – but nothing beats a generous smear of homemade cashew icing to elevate a baked doughnut to greater heights. Vegan food colourings are available pretty much everywhere now (just check the label) and I find pale shades work best here, providing a gorgeous contrast to the delicate freeze-dried strawberries.

1 teaspoon cider vinegar
150ml soy milk
1 tablespoon melted coconut oil
100g golden caster sugar
1 teaspoon vanilla extract
100g plain flour
50g coconut flour
1 teaspoon baking powder
½ teaspoon bicarbonate of soda
pinch of sea salt flakes
1 heaped tablespoon freeze-dried
   strawberries, to decorate

Icing
150g cashew nuts, soaked and drained
   (*see* page 8)
100ml agave nectar
grated zest and juice of ½ lemon
½ tablespoon coconut oil
1 teaspoon vanilla extract
2 tablespoons water
a selection of 3 vegan food colourings

1. Begin by making the icing. Place all the ingredients except your choice of food colourings in a high-speed blender and blitz until completely smooth, scraping down the sides from time to time. Refrigerate for at least 1 hour.

2. Preheat the oven to 200°C (180°C fan), Gas Mark 6. Lightly grease a mini-doughnut tin.

3. Combine the cider vinegar and soy milk in a bowl and set aside for 5–10 minutes to let the mixture curdle. Once curdled, add the coconut oil, sugar, vanilla extract and 1 tablespoon of water and whisk until frothy.

4. Place the flours, baking powder, bicarbonate of soda and salt in a large mixing bowl and whisk lightly to combine.

5. Make a well in the centre of the flour, add the liquid and fold gently to form a wet dough.

6. Transfer the dough to a piping bag and pipe it into the prepared doughnut tin to fill the moulds, smoothing them with the back of a spoon. Bake for 12 minutes, or until lightly golden, then transfer to a wire rack to cool for 1–2 minutes before removing from the tin and leaving to cool completely.

7. Remove the icing from the refrigerator and divide it between 3 mixing bowls. Add 1 teaspoon of food colouring to each bowl and whisk vigorously with an electric whisk until the icing is light and fluffy.

8. Generously spread the icing over the doughnuts and scatter over the strawberries to finish.

RED PEPPER & HUMMUS MUFFINS

MAKES 6 LARGE MUFFINS

I have been keeping this muffin recipe close to my chest for years, with many versions having been consumed while I perfected it. I think it was worth the wait. The inclusion of hummus was the breakthrough – it not only binds everything together but gives these muffins a real depth of flavour. You could make your own but I actually find that shop-bought hummus is best in this particular instance. While I've gone for strong white bread flour, spelt would also be stellar. And don't be afraid of over-filling your tin – the bigger the muffin-top, the better.

1 teaspoon cider vinegar

150ml soy milk

2 tablespoons olive oil

1 red pepper, cored, deseeded and diced

2 spring onions, sliced

175g strong white flour

1 teaspoon baking powder

½ teaspoon bicarbonate of soda

½ teaspoon sea salt flakes

¼ teaspoon black pepper

20g chopped fresh coriander

3 tablespoons hummus

1 tablespoon maple syrup

1. Preheat the oven to 200°C (180°C fan), Gas Mark 6. Line a 6-hole muffin tin with muffin cases or strips of baking paper.

2. Combine the cider vinegar and soy milk in a bowl and set aside for 5–10 minutes to let the mixture curdle.

3. Heat 1 tablespoon of the olive oil in a frying pan over a medium heat. Add the pepper and spring onions, season and sauté until just beginning to soften. Remove from the heat and set aside until needed.

4. Place the flour, baking powder, bicarbonate of soda, salt, pepper and chopped coriander in a large bowl and whisk to combine.

5. In a separate bowl, whisk the hummus, maple syrup, soy milk mixture and remaining 1 tablespoon of olive oil together until smooth.

6. Make a well in the centre of the flour. Add the hummus mixture together with the sautéed peppers and spring onions and gently fold together.

7. Divide the mixture evenly between the muffin holes and bake for 20 minutes until risen and lightly golden.

8. Transfer the tray to a wire rack and leave the muffins to cool slightly before easing them from the tin. Leave to cool completely, then transfer the muffins to an airtight container and enjoy when you like (they will keep for up to 1 week).

PUMPKIN MUFFINS

MAKES 6 LARGE MUFFINS

As soon as autumn makes an appearance I unleash my pumpkin-baking prowess. These are months I relish and I always feel the need to make the most of the season. Right up until Thanksgiving (a tradition we've adopted since living in Chicago) my house is filled with the scents of cinnamon and nutmeg, usually emanating from some sort of baked good. These simple pumpkin muffins are surprisingly versatile and can be enjoyed in a multitude of ways: if eating them hot like this, I prefer to leave them unglazed and spread them with coconut or dairy-free butter, though they are also great drizzled with a sweetened version of my Goes-with-Everything Tahini Sauce (*see* page 151). I also like to stir fruit through the batter before baking – apples are good, as are cranberries but I think my favourite is probably pear. Have a play around, see what you like best and be sure to make the most of those pumpkins.

1 small–medium-sized pumpkin, halved and
   seeds removed
175g spelt flour
75g golden caster or light brown sugar
2 teaspoons baking powder
1 teaspoon ground cinnamon
¼ teaspoon ground ginger
¼ teaspoon freshly grated nutmeg
¼ teaspoon allspice

pinch of sea salt flakes
3 tablespoons olive oil
1 tablespoon maple syrup
½ tablespoon black treacle
1 teaspoon vanilla extract
4 tablespoons soy milk
1 tablespoon water
coconut butter or dairy-free margarine,
   to serve

1. Preheat the oven to 220°C (200°C fan), Gas Mark 7.

2. Arrange the pumpkin halves skin-side down on a baking tray, pour over 150ml of water (this will prevent it from sticking to the bottom and will help it steam slightly) and roast for 1 hour, or until the skin is easily pierced with a sharp knife. Remove from the oven, turn the pumpkin halves over and leave to cool for 10–15 minutes, then scoop out the soft flesh and leave to cool completely before transferring to a blender and whizzing to a fine purée. Transfer to an airtight container and set aside until needed.

3. Reduce the oven temperature to 200°C (180°C fan), Gas Mark 6 and grease and line a 6-hole muffin tin with muffin cases or strips of baking paper.

4. Whisk the spelt flour, sugar, baking powder, spices and salt together in a large bowl.

5. In a separate bowl, combine 100g of the pumpkin flesh together with the olive oil, maple syrup, black treacle, vanilla extract, soy milk and measured water.

6. Make a well in the centre of the flour, pour in the pumpkin mix and gently fold until just combined, ensuring not to overwork the mixture.

7. Divide the mixture evenly between the muffin holes and bake for 20–25 minutes until risen and lightly golden. Serve hot with coconut butter or dairy-free margarine or leave to cool and keep for up to 1 week in an airtight container.

INDEX

A heartfelt thank you to Octopus for the incredible support, guidance and endless positivity …
it's been a joy from beginning to end. Special thanks goes to Alison for the opportunity to join the
Octopus family – I couldn't hope for a better editor. Huge thanks also goes to Jonathan for his incredible
artistic prowess in bringing this whole beautiful book together, Alex for her beady (and much needed)
grammatical eye, and copy editor extraordinaire Simon. Dream team doesn't even cover it.

To Chris, my agent, thanks for believing in me and helping this little cookbook author have
a bit more faith in herself.

To the fab three (Danielle, Frankie and Ted) who made the food look so darn gorgeous, a colossal
high five … you brought my food to life in a way I couldn't imagine, your collective creativity was
boundless and inspiring.

Thanks to the talented foodie assistants Sophie McKinnon and Charlotte O'Connell …
really lovely working with you, your calming presence was appreciated.

Thank you to Anna Šebestová for her stunning illustrations that complement the design
and food so wonderfully.

To my mother, Marie, for helping me bring this book to fruition despite the difficult circumstances
… know that Dad's presence was with me the entire time, cheering me along. To my sister, friend and
number one fan, Mairead, you have been a rock and a constant source of optimism. Ronan, you joined
our family during our most trying year … grateful to have you in our lives. And to my everything, my
love, my Jason – your unending confidence in my abilities has made all of this possible, so thank you.

An Hachette UK Company
www.hachette.co.uk

First published in Great Britain in 2018 by Mitchell Beazley, a division of
Octopus Publishing Group Ltd
Carmelite House
50 Victoria Embankment
London EC4Y 0DZ
www.octopusbooks.co.uk

Text copyright © Áine Carlin 2018
Design, illustrations & photography © Octopus Publishing Group Ltd 2018

ISBN 978 1 78472 333 0

A CIP catalogue record for this book is available from the British Library.

Printed and bound in China

10 9 8 7 6 5 4 3 2 1

Publisher	Alison Starling
Creative Director	Jonathan Christie
Senior Editor	Alex Stetter
Senior Production Manager	Katherine Hockley
Photography	Danielle Wood
Home Economist and Stylist	Frankie Unsworth
Illustrations	Anna Šebestová
Copy Editor	Simon Davis

ACKNOWLEDGEMENTS